"Jeffrey Hollender and Bill Breen give us the inside scoop on how truly responsible companies out-think and out-perform their conventional-minded competitors. Part manual and part manifesto, *The Responsibility Revolution* delivers a truckload of examples for growing a company that benefits society as well as shareholders. I only wish we had *The Responsibility Revolution*'s real-world lessons when we launched Ben & Jerry's."

—Ben Cohen, co-founder, Ben & Jerry's

"Jeffrey Hollender is a true master of the arts in unifying business with ecology. A rarity indeed, he is one who practices what he teaches."

—Horst M. Rechelbacher, founder, Intelligent Nutrients

"My hat is off to Jeffrey Hollender and Bill Breen for their daring new book, *The Responsibility Revolution*. Drawing on their personal experiences in building the highly successful company, Seventh Generation, and on a wealth of other material, they show with force and eloquence what's required for corporations to transcend the failed promise of 'corporate social responsibility' and give real leadership in building a new economy where people and planet flourish. No more hype and platitudes, *The Responsibility Revolution* is the real item—a Baedeker for businesses that want to be part of a future that works."

—James Gustave Speth, author of *The Bridge at the Edge of the World: Capitalism, the Environment, and Crossing from Crisis to Sustainability*

THE RESPONSIBILITY REVOLUTION

THE RESPONSIBILITY REVOLUTION

HOW THE NEXT GENERATION OF
BUSINESSES WILL WIN

Jeffrey Hollender

Bill Breen

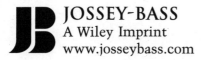
JOSSEY-BASS
A Wiley Imprint
www.josseybass.com

Published by Jossey-Bass
A Wiley Imprint
989 Market Street, San Francisco, CA 94103-1741—www.josseybass.com

Jossey-Bass books and products are available through most bookstores. To contact Jossey-Bass directly call our Customer Care Department within the U.S. at 800-956-7739, outside the U.S. at 317-572-3986, or fax 317-572-4002.

Jossey-Bass also publishes its books in a variety of electronic formats. Some content that appears in print may not be available in electronic books.

Library of Congress Cataloging-in-Publication Data

Hollender, Jeffrey.
  The responsibility revolution : how the next generation of businesses will win / Jeffrey Hollender, Bill Breen.—1st ed.
    p. cm.
  Includes bibliographical references and index.
  ISBN 978-0-470-55842-3 (cloth)
  1. Social responsibility of business. 2. Management—Social aspects. 3. Business enterprises—Social aspects. 4. Business enterprises—Moral and ethical aspects. 5. Social values. I. Breen, Bill. II. Title.
  HD60.H648 2010
  658.4'08—dc22
                                                                    2009043626

Printed in the United States of America
FIRST EDITION

HB Printing 10 9 8 7 6 5 4 3 2 1

CONTENTS

FOREWORD

NOW IS THE TIME

In many ways, the year 2009 marked a historic transition. A free-falling economy put more Americans out of work than at any other time since the Great Depression. The United States' first African-American president took office and cobbled together the biggest economic stimulus package in the country's history. The nations of the world gathered in December for a historic climate negotiation, the first time all major contributors had to acknowledge the growing climate crisis, the need for radical and rapid changes to avert catastrophic possibilities, and the likely costs that future generations will bear.

As dramatic as the year was, it probably offers a representative tableau of the economic, social, political, and environmental turbulence yet to come. According to the World Wildlife Fund, we currently use the equivalent of one and one-third Earths' worth of resources to maintain our lifestyles. If China alone were to reach the rate of U.S. consumption, in terms of natural resources extracted and ecosystems impacted, we would need the equivalent of two Earths. The consequences of such environmental excess and the resultant degradation fall disproportionately on the poor: approximately one billion people do not have reliable access to clean drinking water today; the World Health Organization estimates that number will swell to three billion by 2020. Despite political speeches and growing public concern, global CO_2 emissions in 2006 and 2007 exceeded the Intergovernmental Panel on Climate Change's worst-case scenario; carbon emissions fell slightly in 2008, but only because of the global recession. Clearly, we have not yet begun to slow the drivers of climate change, nor have we seriously started to realign our many social and environmental imbalances.

And yet most talk in the business and public sectors is about getting the economy back to "normal." Although growing numbers of leaders in all sectors are starting to sense the depth and breadth of the challenges that lie ahead, we still assume a return to business-as-usual, albeit with some minor adjustments.

All of this leaves us profoundly ambivalent about the future. On the one hand, we long for real change. Few among us want to live in a way that generates enormous amounts of waste and pollutants, drives farmers around the world into poverty, depletes precious resources like fish and forests more rapidly than nature can replenish them, destroys species and ecosystems, or heats up the planet. On the other hand, we fear that a future fundamentally different from the past is not truly possible. Consequently, we have little collective will to follow a better path.

Insofar as business is one sector that must help take a lead in building a better future, the burgeoning corporate social responsibility (CSR) movement gives us reason to hope. But it, too, has been mired in this same ambivalence. Many executives now concede that companies that focus narrowly on their own bottom line and ignore their larger social and environmental impacts invite activists' ire and put their profits at risk. Consequently, more and more multinational corporations are turning out glossy CSR reports and are creating senior staff positions dedicated to corporate responsibility. Not surprisingly, CSR consulting is now a booming business.

Then again, I doubt most people would hold out present CSR programs as a grand success story of transformation accomplished. Despite CSR's best efforts, for the most part, we still make the wrong products, powered by the wrong energy, driven by the wrong business models. A small number of corporations are starting to internalize the truly strategic implications of the changes that are looming, but even these few leading enterprises are far from truly integrating an expansive business mission into their daily operations.

I can see only two things that will shift this state of affairs: a different vision of the future that is more inspiring than the status quo, and a new consensus on what it will take to move toward it. It is because of this that I think Jeffrey Hollender and Bill Breen's new book could not be timelier.

No one has drafted the definitive map of the new territory where truly sustainable enterprises are built, but Jeffrey Hollender can certainly lay claim to having spent as much time as almost anyone exploring the terrain. He cofounded Seventh Generation twenty-one years ago on the premise that merging social and environmental justice with product, market, and management innovation is good business.

Today, Seventh Generation is a nationally recognized consumer-goods company that markets a complete line of household products, from recycled paper towels and tissues to biodegradable detergents. The company's innovative way of using products to educate consumers on how to create a healthier home and biosphere is pioneering a new field of responsible marketing, which has helped make Seventh Generation the nation's fastest-growing brand of natural home and personal-care products. Its commitment to building networks of trusted business partners, or "SEDRs" (self-extending developmental relationships), has helped it grow large while staying small. In 2008, Seventh Generation reported nearly $150 million in annual sales, which it achieved with a workforce of fewer than one hundred and fifty—a sales-productivity ratio that any business would envy.

In *The Responsibility Revolution*, Hollender and business writer Bill Breen lay out what they believe are the basics of a vision of a better business, one that operates in greater harmony with its environment and offers a more exciting and meaningful place to work. The vision blends principles and practices—like understanding the challenges that come with creating a sense of purpose and what it takes to integrate that mission into an enterprise's day-to-day work. The key is to keep building capability along both dimensions, increasing genuine commitment and the skills to deliver on that commitment.

For example, Hollender is a deep believer in transparency, an idea that most businesses embrace in principle but find terrifying in practice—for good reason. A company that reveals its demerits as well as its merits opens itself up to a never-ending and invariably humbling journey of examining facts, listening to others' views, reflecting, and learning. Those organizations that do it well build a culture that embraces high levels of self-criticism and a willingness to challenge management's most cherished beliefs—including its privilege to make decisions behind closed doors. Such a culture inevitably extends to all members of the organization and beyond, including those who are neither employees nor experts in the business.

Like the other dimensions of change that Hollender and Breen explore, none of this is quick or easy. An organization that benefits society as well as shareholders requires leaders at all levels who never stop reflecting on who they are and who they want to be, who can blend their own personal vision with those who see the world differently, who tell the truth about obstacles and recognize their own personal responsibility in creating them, and who know there are no final answers or formulas. Building a responsible company takes, literally, forever.

Richard Beckhard, one of the pioneers in the field of organizational development, used to say, "People do not resist change, they resist being changed." We will know we have really begun this journey when leaders at every level summon the clarity and passion to follow their own minds and hearts in creating business anew. This small book will likely make a big contribution on both fronts.

Peter M. Senge
September 2009

PREFACE

THE RESPONSIBILITY REVOLUTION:
OUR MANIFESTO

Twenty years ago, when Seventh Generation told executives at the old Fort Howard Paper Company that we wanted to market bathroom tissue made from unbleached recycled fiber, they laughed. Even then, the paper industry made tissue with recovered wastepaper—but that was a well-kept secret. That we wanted to announce this to our customers, at a time when "recycled" was equated with "rejected," was judged nothing short of madness.

We went on to do many more things that broke with business convention. We criticized our own products. We gave stock to all our employees. We limited senior management's salaries to no more than fourteen times the earnings of our most junior staffer. Dogs roamed through our Burlington, Vermont headquarters. One office was turned into a nap room. Instead of promoting our products, we endorsed Bill Clinton and Al Gore on the cover of our mail-order catalog.

Always more activists than hawkers of products, we were part of a small band of companies that set out to change business. Together with Ben & Jerry's, just up the road from us, and along with mavericks like the Body Shop, Patagonia, and Working Assets, we spent endless hours talking about business's untapped potential for doing good.

To this day, Seventh Generation has continued to act as a laboratory for designing, through many trials and more than a few errors, an authentic and transparent model of corporate responsibility. It's a place where we try almost anything and stop at nothing. We hired a "director of corporate consciousness." We built the Seventh Generation Nation of conscious consumers, now almost two hundred and fifty thousand strong. We don't have a PR director; we have a "conversationista." We don't have a brand manager; we have a "brand mother." Our corporate manifesto is not about quarterly earnings, return on equity, or market share; it's about creating a just and equitable world, inspiring conscious consumption, and building coalitions that create new possibilities. Our name comes from the Iroquois, not an ad agency.

Today, green products are as plentiful as businesses that define themselves as "socially responsible." You can find Kimberly-Clark's Scott Naturals in any Walmart, Clorox's GreenWorks in Target, organic Cheerios in Safeway, "clean coal" and "greenhouse-gas-friendly" nuclear power promoted in Washington, and hybrid SUVs at an auto dealer near you. Has our movement been co-opted? Has it lost its heart and soul?

Certainly, corporate responsibility is more visible than ever before. It delivers good press, and even skeptics can see that environmental improvements and energy efficiencies reduce costs. But despite the thousands of corporations that have signed codes of conduct promising good behavior, the events that triggered the brutal recession of 2008–2009 demonstrate that far too few companies are moving in a truly "responsible" direction. And so we need a revolution. We can no longer afford incremental improvements, fine-tuning, or easy upgrades in the way we execute on corporate responsibility. We've run out of time for the go-slow approach. As Peter Senge and his coauthors proclaim in their recent book, this revolution is a "necessary revolution."[1] Without it, the brand called business will continue to suffer.

Most revolutions, of course, end badly, with the protagonists bloodied by their own intemperance. Many a revolutionary has championed a radical business agenda that attempts to overthrow the status quo, but ultimately has been smacked by a backlash (reengineering, for example), undercut by inflated claims (the dot-com revolution), or brought down by hubris and unbridled risk-taking (the financial-derivatives mania). We believe this transformation is different, because it's as much an *evolution* as a revolution. It is built on a resilient business case. It involves sweeping change, but change that starts in our minds—in wiping away the deeply ingrained, almost unconscious way that we've come to narrowly define the purpose of business.

For too long, despite business's supposed embrace of corporate responsibility, the vast majority of companies have deemed it entirely acceptable for their activities to diminish society and impair the environment. What matters most is that stock prices rise and executives "win." Again and again, the interests of a few are deemed more vital than the welfare of the many. Although we concede that putting the good of society ahead of the profit motive still doesn't even enter into most executives' frame of reference, we believe those old mental models will change. Indeed, among a small but growing vanguard of business revolutionaries, they already have changed. And when ideas change, our future changes with them.

When we set out to write this book, we knew it was far bigger than any one company's story, including Seventh Generation's. Other insurgent companies are innovating powerful ways to build market share and grow revenue by confronting confounding social and environmental challenges. When we reached out to their founders and CEOs, the response was overwhelmingly positive. We were granted access to all kinds of responsible revolutionaries, including a number who don't often give interviews. They reasoned that if this book's readers can improve on their successes and learn from their mistakes, more businesses might finally get serious about corporate responsibility.

So as you move through the book, you will encounter a potent mix of veteran revolutionaries, as well as some that aren't often associated with the corporate responsibility tribe. Each offers new models for building the kind of companies that will thrive in the emerging sustainable economy.

There are pioneers like Patagonia, Organic Valley, and Seventh Generation, who have pushed past the incremental approach to advancing sustainability. They have continued to innovate and build on past successes, often redefining the revolution's leading edge.

There are big brands like Nike and Timberland, who long ago had change forced upon them and now are leveraging sustainability as a powerful force for innovation in new and surprising ways.

We've included European bellwethers like Marks & Spencer and Novo Nordisk, who are raising the bar on what's possible and forcing competitors to respond.

Then there are the revolutionary parts of more conventional corporate giants like eBay and IBM, who are applying their powerful resources to solving some of society's most vexing problems.

Finally, there are the outliers, like Etsy and Linden Lab, who represent the first iterations of imminent change.

These business insurgents would be the first to concede that no company, including their own, has fully embedded the responsibility revolution into all that it does. To varying degrees, each of the companies featured in this book is a work in progress. Yet each offers promising ideas for building financially, socially, and environmentally sustainable organizations. Although there is no single road map for forging a business driven by such a mission, these innovators have laid out a series of navigation points that show the way. It's up to each of us to pick the path that best fits our circumstances, using their experiences as our inspiration.

For too long, our definition of what constitutes "responsible" corporate behavior has been dangerously narrow and timid. We've often glorified our efforts to be a little less bad, hailing them as examples of important change. We've cloaked our irresponsible behavior with "cause-related" marketing campaigns, and celebrated "progress" that often was little more than compliance with existing regulations. We've printed millions of corporate responsibility reports that are rife with pretty pictures but way too thin on setbacks and failures.

The responsibility revolution is about more than cutting carbon, reducing energy use, monitoring factories, or donating to charities. It's about reimagining companies from within: innovating new ways of working, instilling a new logic of competing, identifying new possibilities for leading, and redefining the very purpose of business.

Consequently, we've drawn on the best thinking not only from the corporate responsibility arena, but also from the realms of strategy, leadership, and management. Others, to whom we are indebted, have developed some of this book's core principles. (We will acknowledge them as we present their ideas.) Our intent is to show how an emerging breed of business revolutionaries is turning theory into practice and building organizations that grow revenue by contributing to the greater good. This is a book about change, but it seeks to help companies change on the inside—change their priorities, the way they organize, how they compete, and the way they interact with the world.

We fully concede that many companies, perhaps even most companies, won't willingly alter their behavior. But they will change nonetheless, and it won't be because they've suddenly seen the light. It will be because massive numbers of consumers, a spreading swarm of competitors, values-driven employees, and even that laggard indicator, the federal government, makes them change. Change is under way. The responsibility revolution spreads. Perhaps you've seen the insurrection begin to roil your industry, and you're determined to get out in front of it. If so, welcome to the cause.

THE
RESPONSIBILITY
REVOLUTION

THE RESPONSIBILITY REVOLUTION TAKES OFF

It was the summer of 2009, and the world's economy was still struggling to break free from the Great Recession's chokehold. Certainly, the financial industry was the last place that anyone would look to find a business success story. If anything, big banks epitomized much of what had gone wrong in the economy and in society over the past few years. With all of their ethical breaches and criminal wrongdoing, and the billions wiped from their balance sheets, banks revealed business's dark underside. It was not a welcome sight.

So it was surprising that in the midst of the Great Recession's gloom, a bank showed us a bit of business's bright side. Yet that's exactly what Triodos Bank N.V. did in June 2009, when it released its 2008 earnings review.

Based in the Netherlands, with a network of offices throughout much of Western Europe and slightly more than EUR 3.7 billion under management, Triodos[1] is largely ignored by Wall Street's behemoths. But in a year when the Street's failures nearly brought down the global economy and credit markets hit the deep freeze, Triodos Bank's income rose by 25 percent, and its loan portfolio jumped by the same margin.

Triodos delivered those stellar results by financing *only* sustainable projects and businesses—in all, more than nine thousand social and environmentally beneficial initiatives in 2008. No matter how impeccable your pedigree or rock-solid your business plan, if your venture doesn't positively contribute to the environment or society, you don't stand a chance of obtaining a loan from Triodos. By investing solely in enterprises that engage in renewable energy and organic farming, microfinance and fair trade, Triodos aims to steer economies in a more sustainable direction. Profits follow. Despite the busts that regularly buffet the banking industry, Triodos has never recorded a quarterly loss in the three decades since its founding. "As a bank, our first priority is to maximize sustainability," Triodos' chairman and chief executive, Peter Blom, told us. "Within that model, we want to maximize returns for shareholders. But sustainability comes first."[2]

To the conventional-minded, putting values before profit is an upside-down way to build strategy—and an all-downside way to spur sales. It sounds extreme, even anarchic. Perhaps Triodos Bank's resilience and results might give skeptics cause to reset their thinking. For this Dutch bank signals that "corporate responsibility"[3] (CR) may well be undergoing a period of unprecedented "punctuated equilibrium"—the controversial theory promulgated by the renowned paleontologist Stephen Jay Gould.[4] He posited that evolution proceeds mostly slowly, but not always steadily—that it is sometimes inter--rupted by sudden, rapid transitions, in which species decline and are supplanted by entirely new forms. Triodos Bank's consistently positive performance, which grows out of its mission-first approach to investing, is but one more prominent piece of evidence that corporate responsibility is entering a period of dramatic, accelerated change in its own evolution. What new shapes CR is about to take on, we are just now

beginning to understand. But we know this much—corporate responsibility is undergoing a change that's as revolutionary as it is evolutionary.
Consider the evidence:

An emerging breed of values-driven companies—some new, some
well established—is building a better form of capitalism.

A new generation of values-driven leaders has kicked over the alpha
capitalists' argument that "the only business of business is business."

Old-guard notions about "culpability" and "accountability" are
being subsumed by the vanguard's requirement to act authentically and
transparently.

Bloodless buzzwords like "corporate responsibility" and "eco-
efficiency" are being supplanted by a new vocabulary—"corporate
consciousness," "resource intelligence," "social innovation"—that
aspires to capture our real-world experiences.

Above all, tomorrow's bellwether organizations are moving beyond
the moralist's dictum to be less polluting, less wasteful, "less bad."
They are striving to meet the innovator's imposing imperative to be all
nourishing, all replenishing, "all good."

This moment of punctuated, accelerated change affects all of us
in business. It will determine how tomorrow's companies organize,
strategize, and compete. It will reveal new leaders and expose the
phonies and purveyors of greenwash. It will redefine business's
obligations to society and reconfigure the sources of growth and
competitive advantage. And it will require us not only to anticipate the
end of corporate responsibility as we've known it, but also to imagine
the whole new models that will replace it.

RESPONSIBLE REVOLUTIONARIES EMERGE

This first decade of the twenty-first century has brought with it the
necessary catalysts for sparking an enduring period of accelerated change
in corporate responsibility's evolution: our unmitigated ambiguity about
the future, combined with unwavering certainty that business can do
better. We've endured a global recession and the angry backlash that followed: fear over the millions of lost jobs, outrage over CEOs' enormous

pay packages, the gnawing belief that executives cooked the books and scorched the environment, the rough evidence that we were let down by so many of our so-called leaders. Corporations and the people who ran them were widely regarded as covetous and uncaring; the brand called capitalism suffered accordingly.

It's no wonder, then, that although it's fashionable for folks in the C-suite to proclaim their commitment to "corporate responsibility," such talk often rings hollow. Yet a growing number of business leaders are pushing toward a more generous form of capitalism, one that consciously works for the common good. Adam Smith, best known for *The Wealth of Nations,* asserted in his other remarkable book, *The Theory of Moral Sentiments,* that although man is indeed selfish, "... there are evidently some principles in his nature which interest him in the fortunes of others, and render their happiness necessary to him, though he derives nothing from it, except the pleasure of seeing it."[5] Building on Smith's notion that the desire for social approval is at least as powerful a motivator of human behavior as the self-serving desire to win at all costs, if not more so, more and more business innovators are envisioning a different kind of company: a company for which making profits is a way toward the greater goal of responding to social and environmental challenges.

By seeking to contribute to the well-being of society and the environment as well as its bottom line, the enlightened corporation summons instincts—empathy and generosity, passion and ambition—that are more than merely mercenary. It thereby seizes on a more resilient business model than the profit-first strategies that it vies with. Over the long run, companies that really are responsible will surpass their profit-fixated peers.

This fundamental shift from the "for-profit" model to one that's "for-purpose (and profits)" was heralded long ago by such seers as Peter Drucker, who opined that "every social and global issue is a business opportunity just waiting for the right kind of inventive entrepreneurship, the right kind of investment, the right kind of collective action."[6] The right moment for Drucker's vision has been a long time coming, but it has most certainly arrived. Although the notion that there's good business in confronting society's most vexing challenges was once dismissed by many as a misguided mantra, it has now entered the mainstream of business thinking.

Two critical pieces of evidence for this claim came from two of the foremost champions of conventional capitalism: Bill Gates, the cofounder of Microsoft, and Lee Scott, the ex-chief of Wal-Mart.[7] In January 2008, at an annual meeting of Wal-Mart employees and suppliers, Scott made sweeping commitments in his social manifesto to reduce the company's energy use and improve labor conditions in its supply chain. The very next day, in a speech to the World Economic Forum in Davos, Switzerland, Gates heralded the rise of a "creative capitalism" wherein "more people can make a profit, or gain recognition, doing work that eases the world's inequities."

The most remarkable thing about Gates's and Scott's speeches was that they simply underlined what many business leaders had already concluded: that a whole host of economic and societal pressures—and opportunities—are pushing corporations to embrace a model of a more expansive business purpose. In a 2007 report by McKinsey, the global consultancy, more than 90 percent of the CEOs surveyed said they are doing more to push environmental and social strategies into their operations than five years ago.[8] *The Economist,* which once derided corporate responsibility as a "do-gooding sideshow," conceded in a January 2008 article that "CR is booming" and "few big companies can now afford to ignore it."[9] Even *Forbes,* the self-described "Capitalist Tool," has boasted of a surprising turnaround in its profits-centered ethos. "Do corporations exist solely to maximize their bottom lines?" the magazine asked, in a subhead to a March 2008 article. Its emphatic reply: "We don't think so."[10]

Why is this different from the drumbeat for corporate accountability that started at the beginning of the decade, after the Enron, WorldCom, and Tyco debacles?

- Companies, in the wake of such scandals, must now work harder to protect their reputations.
- Global brands, which are battling to crack markets all over the world, are now expected to perform a social role.

- Customers, thanks to the Internet, now have more power than ever before—the power to scrutinize companies' activities and to organize boycotts at the slightest sign of misbehavior.
- The body politic, seared by Ponzi schemes and the meltdown in financial markets, is punishing "bad companies" and demanding that all companies "do good."
- Employees now expect companies to adopt a purpose that's bigger than profit—a key factor in the competition for A+ talent.
- Nongovernmental organizations (NGOs) are growing exponentially and are relentlessly pushing companies to contribute to society.
- Stakeholders are pressuring institutional investors to adopt strong principles of governance and a responsible investing strategy.

People across the political spectrum are concluding that despite the U.S.'s government bailouts of Wall Street and the U.S. car industry, business is still fast enough and nimble enough to innovate solutions to some of the world's thorniest problems. Two proof points among thousands: Unilever's pledge to certify as sustainable all of its Lipton tea bags sold globally, which promises to lift one million African tea growers out of poverty.[11] Or recall the U.S. federal government's feeble response to the devastation caused by Hurricane Katrina. Wal-Mart, with its world-class logistical operation—along with the help of countless individual volunteers and non-profits—proved to be the *real* first responder.

More than anything, climate change is forcing business and society itself to rethink everything, from transportation to energy sources to geo-politics to cities. When the oil baron T. Boone Pickens attacked the United States' petroleum-based economy as a risk to national security, it was clear that minds have changed. Formerly fringe notions that business should be environmentally and socially sustainable have moved to the mainstream—and the business landscape has been fundamentally transformed.

TO BUILD A BETTER CAPITALISM

The voices of the business establishment have come to recognize eight key drivers (described in this section) that make responsible corporate behavior an imperative. Not only are they persistent, they are predominant, and they will endure for decades to come. But although these über-capitalists are putting real heft behind the movement to build a better form of capitalism. The next generation of entrepreneurs is pouring on the accelerant and lighting the match. They have heard the voices of visionaries such as the pioneering ecologist and biologist David Suzuki, who has perturbed many an industrialist with his observation that "the industrialized world has only 20 percent of Earth's population but uses more than 80 percent of the resources and produces more than 80 percent of the toxic waste."[12] They accept Suzuki's argument that our conspicuous consumption is "using up what our children and our children's children should expect to inherit." They reject the notion that business, in its present form, can sustain us, so they too are committed to remaking business. Forged by the old guard and the vanguard, good companies are coming to the fore because . . .

1. *They are preparing for global climate change's threats and opportunities.* The political push to stamp a higher price on fossil fuels through emissions caps or a carbon tax will make clean technologies and renewable energy a necessity for any manufacturer that hopes to stay competitive. American venture capital firms invested more than $2.6 billion in green businesses during the first three quarters of 2007, the highest level ever recorded. That capital quickly paid off: revenues from companies in solar energy, wind, biofuels, and fuel cells jumped from $40 billion in 2005 to $70 billion in 2007. Although the global recession temporarily dampened the surge, VC investments in clean technologies and renewables began rebounding sharply in the second quarter of 2009. Speaking before a meeting of green-tech execs in Boston, Kleiner Perkins's Bill Joy described the future this way: " . . . energy and green technology is the largest economic opportunity we've seen so far this century."[13]

2. *They possess built-in "insurance" that protects a company's most valuable asset: its reputation. Fortune* has calculated that "intangible assets"—patents and trademarks, as well as all the knowledge, creativity, and consumer relationships that ultimately enhance an organization's reputation—represent 75 percent of the total value of the average U.S.

business. A company can buy insurance to safeguard its physical assets. But when more than half of the worldwide respondents to the 2009 Transparency International's Corruption Perceptions survey believe the private sector is dishonest, only the badge of good corporate citizenship can burnish a company's far more valuable reputation.

3. *They are powerful magnets for high-end talent.* In their "Owner's Manual" for shareholders, Google founders Larry Page and Sergey Brin proclaimed that, "Talented people are attracted to Google because we empower them to change the world." As the author and business strategist Gary Hamel has argued, in too many companies, employees aspire to no bigger ambition than hitting their numbers—not much of a stimulant for overachievers. Whether it's Google's effort "to organize the world's information,"[14] Whole Foods' drive to "improve the health and well-being of everyone on the planet,"[15] or Genzyme's aspiration to "innovate on behalf of people with serious diseases,"[16] an audacious desire to create something of consequence is a powerful lure for smart people who thrive on cracking the code on problems that matter.[17]

4. *They summon extraordinary contributions from their employees.* Companies that are organized around a sense of mission not only attract the best human capital, they often yield the best results, because they inspire people to bring all of their imagination and inventiveness to work each day. Most of the organizations that make *Fortune*'s annual "100 Best Places to Work" list have a core purpose that goes above and beyond the bottom line. As Hamel notes, purpose elicits passion, which often transforms individual desire into exceptional corporate performance. In his book *Pour Your Heart Into It,* Starbucks chairman Howard Schultz recognized the power of passion when he opined, "Ultimately, Starbucks can't flourish and win customers' hearts without the passionate devotion of our employees."[18] One piece of evidence to support Schultz's claim: between 1997 and 2007, those "best places to work" companies delivered more than twice the annualized return of the S&P 500 Index.[19]

5. *They have earned a generous "license to operate" from critical external stakeholders.* A license to operate, with its obligation to meet or exceed a set of legal and regulatory requirements, has long been calculated as a necessary but nettlesome part of the overall cost of doing business.

Today, society increasingly acts as virtual licensors for the operating company. Winning its approval is not just a prerequisite for survival; it's a prescription for success, because it opens the way for companies to start producing real economic and social benefits. Wal-Mart understood this a little too late and struggled to win community approval to site new stores. Google, on the other hand, gets it: the search-engine giant is investing hundreds of millions of dollars in developing renewable-energy technologies. The global community's stamp of approval amounts to a touchstone for Google's brand image and a mark of achievement. As Whole Foods CEO John Mackey once asserted, "If you want to increase shareholder value, you'd better be a positive force in the community."[20] He understands that customers reward companies that contribute to society.

6. *They are recreating their relationships with suppliers.* When activists pulled back the curtain on persistent health, safety, and child-labor violations in the overseas factories of some of America's foremost apparel brands, the targeted companies first reacted with utter predictability: they issued "codes of conduct" for their vendors and dispatched teams of inspectors to expose serial offenders. In its first social-responsibility report, for example, Gap Inc. proudly proclaimed that it had pulled its business from 136 factories that failed to meet its new labor standards. More recently, however, the clothing retailer has come to realize that internal monitoring alone cannot unravel its supply chain's tangled problems, and simply listing the number of offending factories does not inspire the public's trust. In 2006, Gap surprised the business world by identifying, on its Web site, its contract factories, so we could see for ourselves what conditions were like. Rather than simply policing their subcontractors, Gap and Nike—working with union and NGO representatives—are partnering with them, to help them become sustainable and desirable places to work. Contract factories that invest in people and treat their workers well tend to improve efficiency (read: lower prices) and product quality, which grows their business—and helps to grow their customers' business results.

7. *They are well positioned to work with a powerful new "regulatory" force: the NGO.* Over the past fifteen years, NGOs have grown dramatically

to become the eighth largest economy in the world, numbering in the millions and with annual operating budgets of more than $1 trillion. Their accelerating proliferation is rivaled only by their spreading influence. Not so long ago, Wal-Mart viewed NGOs with outright hostility, but learned painfully that it couldn't build a big enough bunker to hide from them. When the retailing giant finally conceded that it needed an environmental strategy, it turned to some of its most zealous critics for help. Wal-Mart's former chief, Lee Scott, contended that NGOs were essential in pushing the company to innovate in such areas as building sustainable fisheries and reducing carbon dioxide emissions. Whereas NGOs once were outsiders who challenged the system, increasingly they act as insiders—a potent part of the system that they are trying to change. No organization is better equipped to partner with this robust new conscience of the marketplace than the conscientious business.

8. *They are harnessing the widespread desire for a new, responsible era in business.* In the November 2008 U.S. presidential election, the majority of Americans voted for change. In the ensuing months, as struggling taxpayers learned to live with less while bailing out Wall Street, they demanded change by rewarding companies that meld economic growth with social justice. *Advertising Age* columnist Jonah Bloom summed up consumers' new expectations thusly: "[C]onsumers, particularly the younger generations of consumers, are moving toward a different way of judging business. They celebrate companies and brands that share their values, rather than have the most muscle . . . [they] have replaced stone throwing and banner waving with the eminently more effective tactic of Web-fueled campaigning and the wielding of their wallets . . . It is difficult for bigger or older brands to emulate this new generation, but they can and must if they want to succeed in selling to today's informed and empowered consumers."[21]

The great green awakening over climate change. The tangible worth of intangible assets. The war for top-grade talent. The impressive power of inspired employees. Communities as corporate licensors. Transparent supply chains. The global swarm of NGOs. Now arriving, the activist global consumer. As these transformational forces reshape the business landscape, insurgent companies that seize on these drives will land on the upside of the change curve and create real value.

RESPONSIBLE COMPANIES, REVOLUTIONARY PERFORMERS

Even skeptics now concede, as mounting evidence reveals, that sustainable companies often enjoy a distinct competitive advantage over their profit-fixated peers and continue to deliver outsized financial results. Here's some real-world evidence.

Between 1995 and 2007, socially responsible investment assets expanded by 324 percent, sharply outpacing growth in the broader universe of investments, which increased by less than 260 percent over the same period. Declared Cheryl Smith, chair of the Social Investment Forum Board: social investing is thriving "as never before."[22] Even during the bust wrought by the Great Recession, investing in socially responsible funds, according to *Time*, grew "at higher rates than ever," to an estimated $2.7 trillion.[23]

Consider also that Clorox, which built its brand on chemical bleach, bought natural-based Burt's Bees for $950 million, a multiple of more than five times the company's 2007 sales. Within two years, Burt's grew into a heavyweight, ranking among the top U.S. "green brands" in a 2009 survey.

Then there's the renewable energy industry. Revenue growth in biofuels, wind power, and solar photovoltaics expanded by 50 percent in 2008, even as tightening credit began to squeeze markets. The future for renewables looks even brighter. The research firm Clean Edge estimated that the three benchmark technologies will leap from $115 billion in 2008 to $325 billion "within a decade."

Organizations that compete outside of the green category are also getting in on the action. A survey by the consulting group A.T. Kearney found that companies committed to corporate sustainability practices achieved "above average" performance in the financial markets during the tough 2008 recession, which translated into an average of $50 million in incremental market value per company.[24]

On the retail front, a Boston Consulting Group survey of nine thousand consumers in developed countries found that *more* shoppers "systematically" purchased green products in 2008, when the global economy was plummeting, than in 2007.[25]

And finally, even the lords of Wall Street are (sometimes) taking sustainability seriously. In 2008, Goldman Sachs created a task force with many of the world's largest financial houses to help that industry put environmental, social, and ethical governance issues at the heart of its investment analysis. Goldman analysts contended that such a perspective amounted to a "good overall proxy for the management of companies relative to their peers,"[26] and thereby signaled their chances of long-term success.

All of these enterprises are at least partly motivated by an eye-opening Goldman finding, which will have even greater relevance as companies dig out of the recession: from 2005 to 2007, organizations that are leaders in leveraging environmental, social, and corporate governance considerations for sustained competitive advantage outperformed global stock funds by 25 percent.

Realizing that corporate responsibility can help them build competitive advantage and burnish their brands, companies are scrambling to proclaim their values and vision, by driving do-good messages into their Web sites, annual reports, and occasionally their advertising.

- More than fifty-two thousand company Web pages highlight the "triple bottom line," signaling that corporations are beginning to account for their net social and environmental impacts in addition to their traditional focus on net income.
- Representatives from more than 4,700 companies in 130 countries have signed the UN Global Compact, pledging to follow its ten principles concerning human rights, labor, the environment, and anti-corruption efforts.
- A growing number of chief executives from the country's biggest companies are lining up at corporate responsibility conferences to pronounce their passion for improving worldwide labor standards or to expound on their company's newfound commitment to creating zero waste.

Given that many executives now see corporate responsibility as a source of competitive advantage—or, at a minimum, as an inescapable priority—we should expect that a sizable number of companies have mastered it. Some have. But although many have done much to improve the social and environmental impacts of their operations, their efforts often fail to deliver the expected results.

GOOD INTENTIONS AREN'T GOOD ENOUGH

To move beyond a strictly bottom-line orthodoxy is to embark on a journey filled with peril as well as promise. Making the shift to a purpose-driven model, in which profits tell you only part of the score, is risky, painstaking work. A company that proclaims its commitment to tackling social and environmental problems in a clumsy or inauthentic way invites cynicism and distrust—and the inevitable backlash. Real responsibility amounts to a land of rich opportunity. But to get there, an enterprise must navigate around six daunting land mines.

1. *Too many options, too little focus.* Corporate responsibility casts a wide net, taking in everything from philanthropic work to treating employees well, from attacking world hunger to protecting the planet. Confronted with such a vast, ever-expanding array of socially worthy activities, many companies are hazy on what to home in on. Their uncertainty reveals itself in the record-breaking proliferation of glossy corporate-responsibility reports and advertising. In 2008, eighty of the UK's top one hundred companies issued CR reports, which typically aim to publicize a company's social sensitivity. Often they fail to make much strategic sense. They'll show the company responding to a swirl of different stakeholder groups and chasing myriad opportunities. But creating a whole lot of busyness is not good business, and ultimately it diffuses the real objective: to deepen the company's social impact.

2. *Commitment at the top, confusion in the middle.* CEOs may have converted to the corporate-responsibility cause, but they're often less than clear on how to connect a purpose-driven strategy with customers and consumers. When middle management is fuzzy on how to meld the vision with the business, big ideas get lost. Although a recent IBM

survey of more than 250 business leaders worldwide found that over two-thirds say they are focusing on corporate social responsibility (CSR) to grow new revenue streams, 76 percent admitted that they "don't understand customers' CSR expectations well." Such a disconnect, the report understated, is "potentially alarming."[27] The best that such companies can hope for is that their managers guess right.

3. *Deputized, then compartmentalized.* Companies typically deputize a corporate responsibility overseer and set up a department from which to grow a CR initiative. But too often, even successful CR efforts fail to break out of the box and aren't allowed to influence decisions across the company. Toyota, for example, led the way in championing green, responsible motoring with its Prius hybrid. But in 2007, the parent company horrified its Prius-driving consumers when it lobbied with Detroit against tougher fuel economy standards. Although the Prius gave Toyota a "green halo," the Japanese carmaker also wanted to move more of its gas guzzlers, like the Tundra, and thereby "beat GM in the big trucks, too," observed the Natural Resources Defense Council's Deron Lovaas.[28] That's what happens when CR is decoupled from the organization's everyday workings: Toyota took a hit to its reputation and lost a tremendous opportunity to do even better by the environment.

4. *Too much friction, too little connection.* In 2008, one of the nation's largest private equity outfits, Kohlberg Kravis Roberts & Company (KKR), turned heads when it joined with the pioneering advocacy group the Environmental Defense Fund (EDF) to measure and improve the environmental performance of all the companies owned by the buyout firm. The alliance made headlines because it was a stellar example of business-as-unusual, for two reasons: (1) the business world is still often skeptical of environmental activism, and (2) many environmental groups are allergic to the notion that "polluters" can be trusted. Fred Goltz, a KKR partner, told the *New York Times* that in joining up with EDF, the company was "trying to be ahead of the curve, trying to see around corners."[29] But all too many business leaders, when they dare to look ahead, see only a dead-end series of disputes with pressure groups, followed by reactive attempts to placate them with some PR in the

guise of CR. And that, in the long run, benefits neither society nor the bottom line.

5. *Massive buyouts, minimal buy-in.* Big-brand buyouts of natural products businesses, such as Clorox's purchase of Burt's Bees, often act as a cover for large corporations hoping to appropriate the virtues of the ethical company so as to rehabilitate their image. More often than not, at least one of the outfits suffers a consumer backlash: the big company gets branded as a greenwasher, the sustainable startup gets slimed as a sell-out. When the French cosmetics giant L'Oreal scooped up the Body Shop, the vociferously ethical hair-and-skin products innovator, the company's pearly white reputation quickly sprouted blemishes. A month after the sale, according to a BrandIndex survey, Body Shop's "buzz" and "satisfaction" ratings among consumers fell precipitously. Consumers perceived that L'Oreal valued Body Shop's growth prospects but not necessarily its values, so they doubted those values would be upheld.

6. *More than enough hype, less than enough honesty.* The market for green products and services has soared dramatically, attracting a flood of offerings from such big brands as Philips Electronics, Kimberly-Clark, Walmart, Staples, and Home Depot. According to TerraChoice, a research firm that operates the Canadian government's EcoLogo program, the total number of products making environmental claims more than tripled from 2006 to 2009. But the surge in green-labeled insect repellents, washing machines, and the like was paralleled by a torrent of green ads, whose purveyors failed to deliver on their promises. A 2009 report by TerraChoice concluded that a stunning 98 percent of environmental advertising claims in North America are "false or misleading." No doubt some (perhaps many) of the ads aimed to hype the product rather than hoodwink consumers. Either way, as the report argues, the effect is often the same: "Greenwashing spreads cynicism and doubt about all environmental claims ... [and] the slowing of real environmental innovation in the marketplace."[30]

Although the opportunity, even the necessity, for organizing companies around a responsible ethos is clear, so too are the obstacles to achieving that ambitious goal. The barriers to such fundamental change are as formidable as they are numerous. To build a better future, leaders and aspiring leaders must first envision their company as an authentically "good company" and then overcome the obstacles to building it.

CORPORATE RESPONSIBILITY 2.0

Not long ago, the vice president of corporate responsibility at a Fortune 500 company confessed that for the past couple of years, she's been trying to change her title. "Corporate responsibility," she explained to us, fails to capture the spirit and the substance of her work, which is to seek out innovations that deliver an ROI (return on investment) to society as well as investors. "I'm all for killing the term 'corporate responsibility,'" she said. "I just can't think of a good replacement."

Hers is not an isolated voice. *Ethical Corporation,* a London-based magazine published by a sustainability think tank, mocks "corporate social responsibility" as a "dreadful term" and asserts that the concept "may be in danger of being sucked back out to sea."[31] *Grist* blogger David Roberts has set his sights on corporate responsibility's homely cousin, *efficiency.* "The word itself reeks of sterile technocracy," he complains. "No wonder it hasn't captured the public imagination."[32] Then there's James H. Gilmore and B. Joseph Pine II, authors of *Authenticity: What Consumers Really Want,* who predict that in a world where consumers now "reject initiatives that merely front as the means to sell more wares," they will increasingly view CSR as a "sham."[33] Perhaps that doesn't amount to a tidal wave of change, but the storm clouds are gathering.

No doubt, it's inevitable that as corporate responsibility gains prominence, its bona fides are sometimes proven bogus. At the time of this writing, the disgraced insurance giant American International Group featured a "corporate responsibility" tab on its Web site, but the link led nowhere, and as we went to press, it had vanished—clear evidence of AIG's real regard for CR. Search for "corporate responsibility" on Citigroup's Web site, and the top result is a bit of puffery on Citi winning a "Best Bank for Corporate Social Responsibility" award in a small eastern European country. How many of the institutions that sparked the

U.S. economy's recent conflagration—AIG, Citi, the mortgage giant Fannie Mae, and the rest—issued corporate responsibility reports that omitted any reference to the reckless bets that caused their downfall? Their demise destroyed millions of jobs, along with the illusion that corporate responsibility actually meant a different way of doing business.

When scandal-racked Fannie Mae can rank first on *Business Ethics* magazine's 2004 list of "100 Best Corporate Citizens," just before federal regulators challenged the veracity of Fannie's financial reporting, we can conclude that too often, CR is simply a way for companies to spin their reputation and burnish their brand. Such companies believed that by checking off the right compliance boxes on a spreadsheet they could become better corporate citizens. Never mind that an authentically good company weaves its aspirations for a better world into the very fabric of its being. For "best corporate citizens" like Fannie Mae, that idea was clearly ahead of its time.

We haven't reached the end of the road for corporate responsibility, but we sense that we are nearing the outer reaches of its evolutionary arc. Moving forward, CR will most likely become a baseline requirement in every company's license to operate, but nothing more. Consumers won't believe that corporate responsibility reports are an indication of greater purpose or higher vision. A listing in the Dow Jones Sustainability Index or inclusion in the portfolio of a socially responsible mutual fund will be more about doing less harm than about acting for the greater good. And that brings us to an evolutionary crossroads or, as Stephen Jay Gould might say, that moment of punctuated equilibrium.

Many companies will continue down the same path, making do-good claims that are little more than marketing pap. They will add CR coordinators who lack real clout. They will treat their CR departments as outliers, filled with "responsibility" ventures for which their operating units feel little or no responsibility. And they will issue glossy reports declaring that they are stellar corporate citizens, while omitting the real costs of their impacts on society and the environment.

At the same time, an insurgent band of revolutionary companies have heard President Obama's call to a "new era of responsibility" and are already thinking well beyond the horizons defined by the Chamber of Commerce. They are committed to twining economic growth with social justice. They view the financial crisis and the climate crisis as once-in-a-generation opportunities to unleash principled behavior for the greater good. For them, values are sources of innovation—opportunities to create products and services that deliver a return on purpose as well as a return on investment. We half expect that good companies will jettison the title VP, Corporate Responsibility, and create a new position that just might speak to the power of innovating for profit and for society: VP, Corporate Possibility—or even SVP, Corporate Consciousness.

We are just beginning to discern the post-CR era, even as a few revolutionary companies are inventing it. But clearly, the future belongs to those in the vanguard of the responsibility revolution—renegade companies that not only bring out the best in employees and stakeholders, but also build market share by committing to a more expansive vision for business.

A BLUEPRINT FOR REVOLUTIONIZING RESPONSIBLE BUSINESSES

There is, of course, no one right way to transform a conventional company into a revolutionary company. It's a process that's marked by experimentation and adaptation and plenty of fast failures before any lasting success. Every company must seek out the formula that works best for its particular culture and industry. Nor is there any business whose every impact is positive. All good companies, including the first wave of "green" companies, are works in progress. But all of the authentically responsible companies we know subscribe to a set of principles—about mission, transparency, working, authenticity, and innovation—that amount to an agenda for building purpose-driven companies that are prepared for the twenty-first century's challenges.

1. *The mission matters.* Responsible companies believe that what you stand for—your purpose and your values—is far more important than the products you make or the services you sell. For them, advocacy is synonymous with strategy—their industry is in dire need of reform and they aim to fix it.[34] That's why Organic Valley, the aggressively

unconventional farmers' co-op that happens to be the nation's second largest maker of organic dairy products, is defying the conventional (and misguided) practices of Big Agriculture itself. When organizations stand for something big—something that truly matters to people—they sharply differentiate themselves from their competitors. You can't make a difference if you're playing the same game.

2. *Dare to wear the see-through.* To be a truly responsible company, you can't be opaque. Thanks to the Internet, customers and NGOs can now watch a company's every move. Good companies invite them to do so. By publicly baring its less than admirable impacts on society and the environment, the transparent company preempts its critics—and takes the first step towards collaboratively fixing its problems. So the Danish pharmaceutical Novo Nordisk, the world's largest maker of insulin, dares to reveal its forays into such controversial topics as animal testing, stem-cell research, and gene technology. In the long run, more eyes ultimately mean more advocates—and fewer difficulties and enemies.

3. *The company is a community.* Work used to be organized in a hierarchy; the C-suite delivered the strategy, and employees executed on it. Today, good companies work like a community. Talented people, animated by the community's sense of purpose, provide the brainpower for generating breakthrough ideas and the firepower for getting them out into the world. Linden Lab, the maker of the wildly successful virtual world called Second Life, understands that by letting associates set their own strategic direction, they act less like employees and more like entrepreneurs. Modeling the company on a community catalyzes people's capacity to create.

4. *Bring consumers inside.* Truly responsible companies aren't monoliths. They know that "no one is as smart as everyone." The more heads they get into the game, the better the chance that they'll make a real difference in the market and in the world. IBM is filled with Mensa-level thinkers, but it doesn't rely solely on them. Big Blue also entices some of the world's brightest minds to help it confront some of the planet's brawniest challenges. Good companies genuinely listen to customers and outside stakeholders. They interact. And a few dare

to put consumers at the very heart of their innovation processes. They leverage people power by giving up control.

5. *Make it real.* Do-good marketing campaigns don't cut it anymore. A company that declares itself to be "sustainable" or "responsible" puts those goals at the very center of all its activities. In the lobby of its London headquarters, the British retailer Marks & Spencer uses a giant electronic ticker to broadcast its performance against 100 social and responsible initiatives. The ticker's implicit message: M&S is genuinely committed to "doing good" and is holding itself accountable for the results. An authentically responsible company's actions align with its words.

6. *Build a corporate consciousness.* No enterprise can truly attempt to embed the sustainable ethos into everything it does without constructing a collective view of what it should be. That requires developing a high degree of clarity about what matters most to the company, then bringing that knowledge to bear on important strategic decisions. For the better part of the past decade, Seventh Generation has endeavored to develop the organization's "collective consciousness" so as to bring a sharper awareness to the way we work and what we seek to accomplish.

All of this starts with learning to ask better questions. No matter what your field of endeavor, the question you ask shapes the answer you get. If you ask, "What can we do to build market share?" you will get a very different answer—and you will create a very different future—than if you ask, "What can we do to build a more sustainable economy?"

For too long, those of us in business have proved adept at posing the first kind of question, but all too inept at considering the second. Here's a question that every business leader should ask, but too few do: "What does the world need most that our business is uniquely able to provide?" Perhaps that question will compel us to explore how we can best respond to the enormous challenges, and the boundless opportunities, that confront us. And even if it isn't the "right" question, it just might lead to the right kind of conversations—deliberations that can help us move beyond *responsibility* and begin to glean the *possibilities* that await.

THE COMPANY TAKES ON A MISSION

2

"DOING WORK THAT MATTERS" MATTERS NOW MORE THAN EVER

The folks at Organic Valley Family of Farms, the nation's second largest organic-dairy business, still call it Dry Thursday. That was the December day when it underscored a fundamental lesson for any company that seeks to act sustainably: the mission means everything.[1]

The story, first recounted in *Inc.* magazine, goes like this: in late 2004, Organic Valley's runaway success yielded a nightmare of a supply crisis. Within a matter of months, consumers had moved en masse toward organic dairy products. Demand quickly swamped supply, forcing Organic Valley to short nearly 40 percent of the orders placed by distributors, infuriating many. One of the biggest drivers of the demand surge was one of the company's biggest customers, Wal-Mart, whose unquenchable thirst for organic milk threatened to drain Organic Valley's supply.

And so, on that memorable Thursday, Organic Valley's aggressively un-CEO-like cofounder, George Siemon, and his management team gathered in the boardroom of the company's hewn-pine headquarters and confronted a company-defining question: should they continue pruning back deliveries for all their customers or instead completely lop off an unlucky few? And if so, which ones? Cut the green grocers who grew Organic Valley in its early days or the big-box retailers like Wal-Mart, which were bringing organic food to the mainstream?

It didn't take long for the conversation to move from sales projections and pricing problems to the larger theme of what values Organic Valley really stood for and how it might continue to live by them.

With his shoulder-length hair and preference for going barefoot in the office, Siemon looks more like the head of a commune—as *Inc.* has observed—than the chief of a sprawling national enterprise. But in the two decades since he and a handful of dairy farmers launched Organic Valley, it had accumulated a portfolio of more than two hundred products and racked up annual sales of more than half a billion dollars—all by putting purpose before profit. Unlike its publicly traded Big Agriculture brethren, Organic Valley's goal has never been to simply maximize shareholder value. It set out to maximize the value of family farms.

After a long, heated debate, Siemon and his team moved to stop doing business with Wal-Mart. It was not an easy decision. Dropping Wal-Mart ran counter to both the logic of business, which is to grow market share, and the logic of the organic-food movement, which is to get organics into places where it's not available. But Siemon reasoned that if Organic Valley became too reliant on one titanic customer, it could easily be pushed into lowering its prices. That would violate its core mission—to provide a stable price and a sustainable business to family farmers. Walking away from Wal-Mart would send a clear signal that Organic Valley would remain loyal not only to farmers, but also to the natural-food stores and smaller retail chains that had helped build its business.

The move dumbfounded the Bentonville behemoth and shocked the retail-grocery industry. Organic Valley soon found itself characterized as the company that had the courage to say "no" to Wal-Mart, that price-slashing menace of small businesses and rural communities. But that wasn't the real story. Organic Valley never milked the David and Goliath myth. In fact, its dairy products have quietly returned to some of the giant's shelves. Dry Thursday's real significance was that it forced Organic Valley to rediscover its true, animating purpose: to grow family farms and, more boldly, to help reverse the industrialization of the nation's food supply. "We weren't being anti-big-business," Siemon told us. "We were just making a values statement on what really mattered to us."[2]

The moral of this story and a key premise for any company that seeks to act sustainably is to serve a larger purpose—whether it's "protecting the health of the family farm" (Organic Valley);[3] to "restore health and extend life" (Medtronic);[4] or "spreading joy for the belly and soul" (Ben & Jerry's).[5] Missions such as these fire people's imaginations and frees a company's capacity to become a force for good in the world.[6] Business, with all of its access to creativity, knowledge, and capital, is uniquely positioned to tackle many of society's most vexing problems, from global climate change and the loss of arable land, to poverty and world hunger, to overpopulation and overconsumption of natural resources. When a company converts from acting as a dispassionate engine of commerce to catalyzing human potential, it seizes on the possibility of bringing real, beneficial change to the world around it. As the strategist and author Jim Collins once put it, such a company "defines success on a very big scale."[7]

THE VALUE OF VALUES

In recent years, it's become more than popular for companies to proclaim the value of their values. Almost every big organization, it seems, has put out a statement of mission-oriented goals and ideals. Typically, such a document hangs in the corporate boardroom and is published in the company's corporate responsibility report. But all too often, the company's values never make it out of the executive suite. They never affect corporate strategy, capital investment decisions, and human resource policies. And they never permeate the culture.

We'll leave it to others to judge, for example, whether Halliburton, the oil field–services giant best known for its misadventures in Iraq, has lived up to its values statement: "To be welcomed as a good corporate neighbor in our communities."[8] Or whether ExxonMobil has met the modest obligation imposed by its mission: " . . . to eliminate incidents with environmental impact."[9] But we can't help feeling that most observers will likely agree: despite setting a remarkably low bar, both conglomerates have managed to duck under it.

Notwithstanding the posers, there remains much evidence suggesting that those companies that find ways to truly live by their values are better able to inspire employees, rally partners, create sustainable economic value, and grab new business opportunities. They tap into that core human desire to identify and fulfill a larger purpose, a notion that is best captured by the Nazi war camp survivor and trailblazing neurologist Viktor Frankl. In *Man's Search for Meaning,* his seminal work, Frankl argued that the pursuit of a worthy goal is not a choice or even a moral requirement, but a fundamental aspect of the human condition. "Life ultimately means taking the responsibility to find the right answer to its problems," wrote Frankl, "and to fulfill the tasks which it constantly sets for each individual."[10]

Organizations that create cultures where people can "find the right answer" are among the most successful. More than a decade ago, the business classic *Built to Last,* by Jim Collins and Jerry Porras, examined the resiliency of such long-standing companies as Johnson & Johnson, 3M, and Procter & Gamble. The pair discovered a powerful sense of mission at each organization, "a set of fundamental reasons for a company's existence beyond just making money . . . [which] should serve to guide and inspire the organization for years, perhaps a century or more."[11]

More recent evidence of the preeminence of values comes from Harvard Business School professor Rosabeth Moss Kanter. Her two-year, in-depth study[12] of a dozen multinationals, including Procter & Gamble, CEMEX, and Banco Real, led her to conclude that in companies where values and standards are widely shared, employees make better decisions, collaborate more effectively, and react to opportunities (and crises) more efficiently. A company is far more likely to win extraordinary contributions from people when they feel they are working toward some goal of extraordinary consequence. Equally important, purpose-driven companies are magnets for partners—from suppliers to customers to the larger community—which heightens the organization's capacity to seize on emerging opportunities.

"Values turn out to be the key ingredient in the most vibrant and successful of today's multinationals," Kanter declares. "[They] are no longer an afterthought ... but a starting point that helps companies find profitable growth."[13]

In fact, a genuine commitment to values can benefit a company of *any* size. At its core, a values-driven company is fundamentally different from its competitors. As William C. Taylor and Polly LaBarre argue in their book *Mavericks at Work*, a company's unique set of values push it to challenge the norms of its industry and to craft an "original blueprint" for its business. To be sure, it exhibits an unmistakable sense of purpose, but it's a purpose with attitude—a purpose that's meant to foment. "Call it strategy as advocacy," they write. "The most powerful ideas are the ones that set forth an agenda for reform and renewal, the ones that turn a company into a cause."[14]

AN OUTFIT WITH A CAUSE: ORGANIC VALLEY FAMILY OF FARMS

Organic Valley illustrates the first principle of purpose: *What you stand for is more important than what you sell.* Its sense of mission grew out of the notion that while all of the issues that swirl around organic food truly matter—protecting the environment, supporting local economies, healthy eating, and humane treatment of animals—the thing that matters most is keeping families on the farm. Given that five million independent farmers have been driven off the land since 1935—and most of those remaining are fifty-five or older—Organic Valley has dubbed the family farmer "an endangered species."[15] Its reformist agenda seeks to reverse that devastating trend.

Sitting astride a hill overlooking the woods and fields surrounding the tiny hamlet of La Farge, Wisconsin—more than forty miles from the nearest interstate—Organic Valley's barn-shaped headquarters is a physical testament to the organization's commitment to preserving a rural way of life. Its roots go back more than two decades, to a time when small farmers were struggling to stay on the land. Many were whipsawed by the wildly volatile pay price they earned for conventionally farmed dairy products, where a 1-percent oversupply could result in a 25-percent drop in the commodity price of milk. A chart tracking the year-to-year fluctuations, from 1989 to 2008, of the pay price for conventional milk looks like a row of shark's teeth, as steep price spikes were often followed by swift, sharp declines.

In the past two decades, most of the family farmers who work the land surrounding La Farge (and areas farther afield) ran up against an untenable choice: get big fast or sell out. The economics for dairy farming grew so dark that in the late 1980s George Siemon, who would later become Organic Valley's chief executive, decided to sell off his herd of cows. In the early 1990s, Jim Miller, who would go on to become a member of Organic Valley's board of directors, lived through the near-death experience of almost losing his farm. The three-hundred-acre spread had been a part of the Miller family since 1852. At Organic Valley, the mission is personal.

Organic Valley's primal connection to family, farming, and the land emboldens its sense of purpose. But the mission's clarity comes from the organization's laser-like focus on maximizing direct payments to farmers.

Organic Valley keeps farmers on the land by never compromising on striking a fair and stable price for organic dairy products. Its ability to pay more to farmers is due in no small part to the fact that the company is really a cooperative, consisting of more than 1,300 family farms in thirty-two states. ("Organic Valley" is the brand name for the La Farge–based Cooperative Regions of Organic Producers Pool, which supplies the dairy products, eggs, and meat that the brand markets and distributes.) By harnessing the power of its brand, which represents its commitment to its farmer-owners, Organic Valley usually has enough clout to demand and deliver its preferred "base-pay price" (the price it pays to farmers) for organics. In fact, over the past twenty years the cooperative has commanded, on average, a 38-percent premium over conventional pay prices. We met with Siemon in his airy corner office, overlooking the winding Kickapoo River. It was a long way from the early days, when he launched the cooperative with seven pioneering dairy farmers. "From the beginning, we were hardcore about setting a price for organic food that would sustain a family-farm culture," he explained. "Nobody in agriculture had been able to produced stabilized prices that reflected the real cost of their goods. But we toughed it out."

Therein lies the second principle of purpose: *When you stand for something different, you will build a different kind of organization.* Organic Valley struck a better deal for farmers by leveraging the scale of its co-op to build a resilient alternative to the massive market for conventionally farmed dairy products. It helped pioneer the markets for organically produced eggs, beef, and pork as well as milk and cheese. And it fashioned a business model that rests on a simple but powerful notion: people will pay a premium for milk and food products that are good for them and good for the environment. From 2005 to 2007, that model helped Organic Valley grow sales by more than $100 million per year. Despite the tough recession, which pushed some consumers back to conventional dairy products, Organic Valley's sales increased by 22 percent in 2008 (it projected a four percent increase for 2009). That's the kind of financial value that an enterprise driven by social values can deliver.

A DIFFERENT KIND OF COMPANY

The cooperative model of business ownership, which dates back to the mid-nineteenth century, has evolved into a globe-spanning movement, with worldwide membership now at roughly eight hundred million people. In the United States, more Americans own memberships in co-ops than own equities in the stock market. Writing in *Strategy + Business* magazine, Marjorie Kelly, a senior associate with the Tellus Institute in Boston, argues that cooperatives are often powerful engines for delivering impressive business and social impacts. "When employee ownership is matched with involvement," she avers, "businesses can achieve results that would be considered near-impossible in conventional companies."[16]

Kelly contends that cooperatives succeed largely because they escape the short-term pressures that keep shareholder-owned companies narrowly focused on nailing quarterly profit targets.[17] But it also seems that values-driven, stakeholder-owned companies reconcile some of the stubborn inconsistencies that plague conventional organizations. Organic Valley does this by using its principles to realign strategic objectives that are often in conflict.[18]

It delivers business value by championing social reform.

Organic Valley's increasing ubiquity—its milk, butter, eggs, cheese, and meats are now sold in more than thirteen thousand stores—has helped it do more than build a business around organic food. The cooperative is quietly defying the status quo customs and practices of Big Agriculture itself—an industry that's certainly ready for reform.

At a time when much of American agriculture is mired in a mindset that relies on petrochemical-based fertilizers, assembly-line feedlots, and genetically modified seed, Organic Valley has imagined a back-to-the-future vision of the family farm that's fit for the twenty-first century. From 2003 to 2008, Organic Valley's sales grew by nearly 153 percent—potent evidence that small and midsize, nonpolluting farms just might leap past our current age of Big Chemistry and Big Oil. The co-op's impressive sales record presents a sustainable counterweight to industrialized farming's (Lite) "Green Revolution," with its brawny compulsion to achieve maximum yields and sky-high harvests. Organic Valley's farmers-turned-reformers are shaping a different kind of future for their industry and reshaping the sense of what's possible for consumers, stakeholders, and entire communities. But while Organic Valley is a co-op with a cause, it's light on the brash attitude. Its marketing plays up the benefits of organics and generally avoids highlighting the demerits of chemical-based agriculture. The reason, explains Siemon, is that they've had to grow organic farming from within the agribusiness's ecosystem. The co-op couldn't win converts to its cause by alienating conventional farmers. "Many of those people are our neighbors. So early on, we never took a real rant against the system. We just quietly went about building our own alternative."

It maintains a powerful sense of what makes it unique, even as it grows by partnering with others.
Organic Valley's core mission is tightly twined with its "core competency": building markets for organic dairy products and winning farmers access to those markets. For all of its other business activities—producing and hauling milk, testing quality, processing cheese and other products—it partners. Essentially, Organic Valley is in the virtual farming business. It leverages outside organizations' skill sets to process and distribute its products. "We're a co-op," says Siemon. "We believe in cooperating."

On a fundamental level, Organic Valley's success depends on the dynamic relationship between its mission-driven farmers, who want to stay on the land, and its mission-driven associates, who want to grow a sustainable business. Neither can succeed without the other. Beyond those two critical groups, Organic Valley relies on three spheres of partners to scale the business.

• The innermost sphere consists of *likeminded stakeholder groups,* such as the National Farmers Organization, a non-profit that seeks to benefit family producers by negotiating better sales terms for their commodities. In Organic Valley's fledgling years, the NFO gave it financial and logistical support and most importantly, the credibility to strike deals with processing plants. Even today, of the eighty-five cheese processors Organic Valley works with, it owns just one.

• The next sphere is made up of *business partners* such as Stonyfield Farm, the world's largest organic yogurt company. For many years, Stonyfield (now a division of the French multinational Groupe Danone) has worked with Organic Valley on negotiating sustainable pricing, forecasting supply and demand trends, and striking a long-term contract to help expand each other's businesses while advancing a shared vision of sustainable, organic family farming. The two organizations partner for purpose and for profit—and thereby multiply their impact.

• Organic Valley's outermost sphere of partners consists of *consumers*. The organic and local-food movements are in part driven by consumers' desire to reconnect with farming, and Organic Valley has put its farmers at the forefront of its marketing strategy. Its first slogan, "farmers and consumers working together for a healthy Earth," was a little heavy on the granola. But it did signal that Organic Valley recognized, early on, that to grow the business it would have to build a relationship between the farmers at the beginning of its value chain and the shoppers at its end. Farmers and consumers, working in conjunction with each other and government regulators, essentially developed the standards for organic dairy products. Consumers have signaled to farmers that they desire milk from cows that *aren't* pumped with antibiotics and growth hormones and that *are* fed grain that's free of pesticides. "Suddenly, farmers and consumers are having conversations," says Siemon. "We've struck a partnership."

It sustains a sense of "control" by building consensus, believing that people with shared values will often find common ground. At Organic Valley, the farmers have a tangible financial stake in the co-op, amounting to 5.5 percent of each member's annual sales. Membership entitles each farm to a single vote, no matter whether the farm runs a herd of forty cows or four hundred. (Votes are typically cast for candidates to the board of directors and for changes in the cooperative's bylaws.) Because Organic Valley's producers have skin in the game (in the form of mission, money, and ballots), they often are highly engaged in working to ensure that the business succeeds.

Organic Valley sets a modest profit goal of 2 percent—just enough to safeguard the business—and awards both producers and associates a bonus if the co-op achieves that goal. The cooperative's members, rather than the cooperative itself, realize real profits. In this way, Organic Valley furthers a sense that those who are working the land and those who are working the business are in it together—that essentially, they share the same future.

Another mechanism for building interdependence: monthly two-hour call-in meetings between Organic Valley's management and executive committees, composed of farmers who represent the product "pools" (such as milk, eggs, and so on) in forty dairy regions throughout the United States. The committees act as frontline scouts who send out early signals on, say, quality issues or changes in the price of feed. This tight linkage between the farmers' "market intelligence" and management's decision-making authority reduces the possibility that small problems could grow into big problems before corrective action can be taken.

Additionally, Organic Valley holds biannual face-to-face meetings with farmers in each of its forty regions. This ensures that producers across the country have a direct voice in shaping the cooperative's strategy and, most critical, in setting the base-pay price for its products. It also increases the odds that producers will buy into management's strategy, as they have had a hand in writing it.

"We never wanted to be a top-down kind of business," says the co-op's dairy director, Jim Wedeberg. "When an initiative comes from the bottom up, it has a better chance of succeeding, because it's got the members' support."

It knows that values are most valuable in challenging times.
The Dry Thursday supply crisis demonstrated that even mission-driven organizations like Organic Valley must sometimes stop, recalibrate, and rediscover their core beliefs, especially when major challenges arise. Kanter asserts that crises often "serve to strengthen commitment to values." Collins arrives at a similar conclusion, arguing that in turbulent times, "those who prevail have a set of values that they go back to, no matter what the world throws at them."[19] In a fundamental sense, Organic Valley's Wal-Mart imbroglio forced Siemon and his team to confront a question that challenges every company that seeks to act sustainably: what is the real purpose of our work? The answer, it turned out, is that they are as much in the reform business as they are in the farm business.

Dry Thursday steeled Organic Valley's unalloyed commitment to its values; so too has the recent brutal recession. In the spring of 2009, the ailing economy took a toll on the demand for organic milk, as consumers gravitated toward lower-priced private-label organic and conventional (nonorganic) milk. Some organic-milk distributors responded to the decline by cutting their base-pay price to farmers, which artificially deflated their retail price. But at the time of this writing, Organic Valley was holding firm. Rather than slash its base-pay price or cut its membership, the cooperative required farmers to reduce their output by 7 percent. By maintaining stable pricing, farmers could still plan ahead and avoid devastating market fluctuations. The move, commented Siemon in a prepared statement, "best serves our mission to preserve family farms and safeguard our cooperative."[20]

Looking ahead, no one knows whether a worsening economy will force Organic Valley to reduce its pay price to farmers. No one can safely say whether the co-op will recapture the double-digit growth of just a short time ago or relinquish its lead to larger, better-capitalized competitors. What's certain is that Organic Valley will face challenges from all sides, as the food giants move to cash in on the $9-billion-a-year market for organics. But we also know that the conventional players in the dairy business are going up against more than just a novel business model. They are competing with a very different organization with a very different definition of success—one that chooses to build a mission rather than chase a higher valuation. And that choice just might make Organic Valley an even more resilient enterprise in the years to come.

"The beauty of being a co-op is we'll never sell out," says Siemon. "We don't have this constant threat of exit strategies, mergers, or a change in ownership. All of that is a lot of noise to a business. We don't have that noise. We're a cooperative that's driven by mission. We have permission to think long term."

THE USER'S GUIDE TO BUILDING VALUES: MARKS & SPENCER

Organic Valley's founders built a break-the-mold business model because they began with a break-the-mold set of values. But unless you're launching a startup, starting with a blank slate is not an option. At most established companies, the mission is written into the organization's

EXTREME TEAM: CREATING A PURPOSE-DRIVEN VENTURE AT EBAY

Building a purpose-first venture sounds daunting, and truth be told, it *is*—especially when you work inside a big company. But it's not beyond the capacity of any one individual. Consider the trails blazed by Pryia Haji, a zealous social entrepreneur, and Robert Chatwani, a rising marketing executive at eBay.

Both thirty-somethings live in California's Silicon Valley, and though neither knew the other at the time, both made trips to northwestern India in the summer of 2003. Haji and Chatwani were each struck by the plight of impoverished artisans who lived on just dollars a day because they lacked access to larger markets. Upon their return to the United States, each decided to find a way to connect the thousands of talented artisans in developing countries with the millions of consumers in the United States who buy $55 billion worth of factory-made gifts and household accessories every year.

Chatwani grew his initiative inside eBay. Haji, along with a couple of business-school friends, built a social venture called World of Good Inc. Two years later, they met for the first time and began to forge a partnership that intertwines those two business objectives that are too often in conflict: profitability and responsibility. They call it WorldofGood.com by eBay. It's an online market that aims to sell more ethically sourced goods than any single venue in the world—and substantially raise the income of artisans in developing countries.

"The ROI [on World of Good] is a no-brainer," eBay CEO John Donahoe told us. "Our employees celebrate being part of a company that's having a social impact. A growing segment of our customers really cares about supporting fair trade. And we're providing a platform for people to become entrepreneurs—the core part of our business."[21]

Although Haji and Chatwani took distinctly different paths before finding common ground in their Internet-driven venture, they have remarkably similar insights about building a business that puts mission first.

Start with a Proof-of-Concept Experiment

During his visit to an open-air market in Ahmedabad, Chatwani observed a group of highly skilled jewelers who were paid $3.00 to $5.00 *per day* for their craftsmanship, orders of magnitude less than what the 22-karat gold jewelry sold for in the United States. He wondered what the artisans could make if they had access to the global market and sold directly to consumers. To find out, he bought $700 of jewelry on consignment and resolved to sell it on eBay.

Upon returning to California, Chatwani recruited a writer, designer, and photographer from eBay. Working nights and weekends, they built a first-class product page for the jewelry. After six weeks, they sold it for $1,200. "We showed it was possible to use the Internet to generate unprecedented income for artisans," says Chatwani. "That gave us a reason to start thinking about [fair-trade handicrafts] as an interesting opportunity for the company. The question was, could the experiment work on a far bigger scale?"

Focus the Vision

After graduating from Berkeley's Haas School of Business, Haji spent 2003 doing a lap around the world, exploring ways to exploit markets so as to alleviate poverty. She was encouraged by two robust trends in consumer purchasing. "The incredible surge in the market for fair-trade commodities validated the insight that many U.S. consumers were moving toward products that had a high degree of social consciousness embedded in them," she says. "More broadly, we were seeing powerful trend lines in consumption as a force for action—consumers were spending their dollars to drive companies' behavior."

Haji decided to focus on the four hundred million people in the developing world who work in the "informal sector"—economic activity that is neither taxed nor monitored by a government. A large majority of this segment consists of women, many of whom live on less than $1.25 a day. In 2005, Haji and a couple of friends launched a social venture that aims to build a fair-trade market for handcrafted products, such as gifts and housewares, made mostly by women in developing countries. "We called it World of Good. The brand signals that when you buy this product, you know it benefits people and the planet."

Recruit Powerful Allies
Not long after he sold the jewelry on eBay, Chatwani got a call from Rajiv Dutta, then eBay's CFO, who'd heard about the experiment. Dutta had a keen interest in tapping markets to attack poverty, and he encouraged Chatwani to continue exploring ways for eBay to build a business around socially beneficial, fair-trade imports. Dutta alerted eBay's CEO at the time, Meg Whitman, to Chatwani's project, and introduced Chatwani to Matt Bannick, who was then the president of eBay International. "Our executive team was quite excited with the work," Chatwani recalls. "They created the right environment for us to start thinking seriously about what we could do."

Grow the Business by Growing the Market
Haji's goal was never to simply build a business. She wanted to advance the market for ethically sourced handmade goods — a market whose overall growth was hindered by a lack of broadly accepted fair-wage standards and transparent pricing models. So Haji and some colleagues launched a nonprofit sister organization, World of Good Development Organization, which designed a tool called the Fair Wage Guide. This web-based freeware allows artisans to compare wage standards in 140 countries and thereby achieve real bargaining power with buyers. It also alerts retailers to the fair-trade price for ethically sourced goods, which is typically 20 percent above the country of origin's minimum wage. (Artisans without such associations often make less than 60 percent of their country's minimum wage.) There are now nearly five

hundred companies and organizations around the world using the Fair Wage Guide. "Potentially," says Haji, "it's a standard-setting tool."

Haji is often asked why World of Good didn't license the guide and create a revenue stream off of it, instead of making it freely accessible to anyone on the Web. That view, she insists, is shortsighted. "We believe that as the standards get more transparent, the sector will attract more players. World of Good's position is actually strengthened, because we become champions for the category."

Know Your Vulnerabilities

After winning about $15,000 in seed capital from eBay's senior management, Chatwani ramped up his efforts to develop a business model around the market for handcrafted goods. With a few colleagues, he spent eighteen months meeting with organizations ranging from artisans' groups in India to executives at the World Bank. They concluded that the market was so complex, the best way to build a business was to collaborate with an enterprise that had deep expertise in the sector.

Chatwani settled on World of Good. It had built a robust supply chain in more than thirty developing countries and boasted a healthy offline business through its partnerships with national retailers like Whole Foods Market and campus bookstores. Those relationships could act as a cornerstone for growing the market.

Haji, who was finding it difficult to line up enough retail space to accommodate the surging supply of handcrafted goods, immediately saw the potential in connecting artisans with buyers through eBay. "EBay had the technology and the marketing, and we could provide the know-how to screen these products and meet the supply/demand activity," she says. "EBay could also give us an online market where producers can put up thousands of products that might not otherwise make it to a retail shelf."

In January 2007, the two organizations agreed to start collaborating on WorldofGood.com by eBay.

Maximize the Vision

From the beginning, Haji believed that it was essential to think big. "Meg Whitman asked me to define success. I told her, 'Wouldn't it be great if we could double the amount of ethically sourced goods that are sold in the United States?' That's a $500 million play, which is a huge goal for a social entrepreneur. For someone sitting at eBay, that's entirely possible. So Meg's like, 'Okay, let's aim for something big.'"

Haji's refusal to corral her ambition served her well. EBay was drawn to World of Good precisely because it was focusing on "the entire market for ethically sourced artisan goods, as opposed to their own self-interest as a company competing within that sector," says Chatwani. "World of Good aims to transform this market by bringing efficiency to the entire industry, and that matches up perfectly with eBay's interests."

Permission Not Required

Looking back, Chatwani believes two tactics kept the effort from flaming out. "First, we didn't ask for permission to get started. In large organizations, we're often compelled to ensure that what we're doing falls within the guidance of the company's top executives. But we said, building a business that has a positive social impact is an interesting challenge. Let's do it. If we mess up and have to ask for forgiveness later on, we'll ask.

"The second thing was, we flew under the radar for a while. We kept the team small and learned a lot on our own. Because we stayed clear of distractions, we presented a cohesive strategy."

Hold On to the Big Picture

Haji maintains that regardless of the day-to-day demands of growing the business, it's critical to keep looking ahead. No one can invent the future if they're always mired in the present.

"If everything works the way we hope, we'll harness the market to create opportunities to rebuild communities in the developing world. This model is all about helping consumers make purchases that elevate people's income and opportunities. It's a way for consumerism to be a force for good."

foundation. The values are well entrenched. It's risky for employees to speak out when a company is failing to live up to its purpose. It's tough to overcome the groupthink that the organization is doing the right thing when it actually isn't. Even with senior management's backing, it's extremely challenging to reset the compass and reorient the company. But it's not impossible. Just consider the experience of the Marks & Spencer Group PLC.

Step into the sleek glass-and-steel London headquarters of Marks & Spencer, one of the UK's largest retailers and a British institution, and you quickly spot a giant electronic ticker that wraps around the entire lobby. Bold-faced words ceaselessly crawl across the screen, presenting quick-hit updates on M&S's key performance indicators. But they make no mention of sales, margins, or the fluctuations of the company's share price on the London Stock Exchange.

Rather, as first noted in *The Economist*, the ticker tracks M&S's progress against a sprawling suite of a hundred laudable goals: to become carbon neutral; cease sending its waste to landfills; eliminate the "post-harvest" use of pesticides on its produce: convert twenty million pieces of clothing to Fair Trade cotton; reuse and recycle 125 million clothes hangers; slash the annual use of 250 million plastic shopping bags; ensure that customers, through M&S's partnership with Oxfam, can recycle their used clothing; and much, much more—all of which Marks & Spencer has declared it will accomplish by 2012.

While Marks and Spencer's ticker presents a minute-by-minute news flash on the company's social and environmental performance, the sheer breadth of the company's ambition suggests that it, too, is redefining corporate responsibility, by using its reimagined mission to invent its future.

Based in Paddington Basin, M&S offers thirty-five thousand product lines of food, clothing, and home furnishings (nearly all under its own brand), which are sourced from two thousand worldwide suppliers. The retailer employs more than seventy-five thousand people, who operate more than eight hundred stores in thirty countries and generate roughly £9 billion in sales each year. To be sure, the global recession of 2008–2009, which handed Britain's retail sector its worst downturn in nearly two decades, certainly didn't spare Marks & Spencer. In early 2009, as consumer spending slowed dramatically, it suffered a 40-percent drop in profits. But as we will show, had Marks & Spencer not sought to revive its values and make them the touchstone for the way it does business, it would have fared far worse.

Since its founding in 1884, M&S has grown into one of the United Kingdom's most trusted brands. It is widely respected for its philanthropy[22] and its longstanding effort to make a positive impact in the communities in which it operates—and to inspire other organizations to do the same.[23] In 1998, its ability to offer high-quality goods at fair value helped Marks & Spencer become the first British retailer to earn a pretax profit of more than £1 billion. Then management lost sight of what the retailer stood for, and the company lost its way.

In the early part of the twenty-first century's inaugural decade, M&S came under attack for shifting its clothing production from the UK to contract factories overseas, leaving more than a thousand unemployed British textile workers in its wake. Then the environmental group Friends of the Earth slammed M&S for the potentially harmful (albeit legal) pesticides residue that tainted the fruits and vegetables it sold. The kicker came in 2004. After several years of swooning profits and deteriorating market share, a suddenly vulnerable M&S found itself the target of a hostile takeover. The billionaire investor Philip Green, drawn by Marks & Spencer's still-sterling brand and depressed stock price, offered £9.1 billion for the company. (Green later withdrew his offer.[24])

Even as damning headlines, environmentalists' ire, and the takeover battle swirled all around the company, an ad hoc group of managers launched a series of semi-stealthy, ultra-focused initiatives aimed at pushing M&S to the responsible side of its values. In the early going, there was no grand strategy and almost no executive oversight. The team had enough latitude to lay a foundation that would eventually lift Marks & Spencer to the uppermost ranks of the world's most environmentally and socially ambitious big companies.

M&S's aspirations are now there for all to see—they scroll across that electronic ticker in the retailer's London lobby. But it takes a lot more insight to parse the inspiration and innovation that reside at the heart of the company's mission. Marks & Spencer is far from perfect and certainly not invincible. Even so, it heralds an all-business way for big, established companies to push past the challenges that come with balancing a passion for social and environmental sustainability and a passion for profits.

Challenge: Big brands are magnets for critics.
Solution: Run toward the crisis.

When Friends of the Earth assailed Marks & Spencer for the cocktail of pesticide residues in its produce, the retailer reacted all too predictably. It got defensive, hunkered down, and looked for allies to defend it. After all, even the environmentalists conceded that Marks & Spencer hadn't breached the legal limits. No matter. A recent rash of food scares—mad-cow disease, salmonella in eggs, pesticide-tainted chickens, and more—had worn out British consumers' tolerance for contaminants. Rather than wrangle with the pressure groups, a small group of M&S managers decided to engage them.

"The first meetings were very difficult," recalls Mike Barry, Marks & Spencer's CSR chief, when we met at the company's London headquarters. "There were lots of suspicions on both sides. We were speaking different languages. They wanted to save the planet. We just wanted to sell food products to our customers."[25]

M&S made clear that it vehemently disagreed with the environmentalists' interpretation of the pesticide data. But the High Street retailer ceded the larger point: it was a laggard on sustainability issues. To build credibility, it needed some quick wins. It saw an opportunity in the controversy over the polyvinyl chloride plastic it used in its packaging.

PVC uses a chlorine-intensive manufacturing process that's been implicated in significantly elevated cancer rates. Friends of the Earth and groups such as Greenpeace had targeted PVC as a "poison plastic" linked with a wide range of health and environmental concerns; at the same time, Marks & Spencer had quietly investigated alternatives to the offending substance. So it used its first meetings with the environmental groups to announce it would remove PVC plastic from all of its products and packaging. And it showed it could act decisively by putting a two-year deadline on the pledge. Then it upped the ante. Marks & Spencer vowed to quickly eliminate seventy-nine pesticides, and the company set a target for zero residues in all its foods. Within a year, even as Friends of the Earth continued to attack other supermarket chains, the group cited Marks & Spencer for making a "real commitment" to eradicating pesticides.

Marks & Spencer's initial talks with environmental groups weren't one-off events. In the years since the pesticide flare-up, M&S connected regularly with NGO stakeholder groups in face-to-face, consultant-free gatherings. The company used the meetings to underline its sustainability goals, issue progress updates, share what it's learned and where it's made mistakes, and solicit solutions to tough challenges. The hard work has given rise to hard-won trust. Even so, environmentalists still tear into M&S, as Greenpeace did in 2004, when it accused the company of selling furniture made of wood logged from Indonesia's endangered rainforests. The retailer reacted by redoubling its efforts to work with Greenpeace and fix the problem.

"It's a tough lesson for business—you can't treat an NGO like it's a supplier," says Barry. "Greenpeace is independent. When we get things wrong, it says so. The difference now is, it first gives us the opportunity to make things right."

Challenge: Internal skeptics might stonewall the change-effort.
Solution: Make the business case that doing good means beating
competitors.

When one of Marks & Spencer's chief competitors, the Somerfield
supermarket chain, accused environmental groups of fear-mongering
over the pesticides problem, it came off as just another greedy company that had put its own interests ahead of consumers' health. Never
mind that Somerfield had a legitimate grievance: the environmental
groups had failed to report that residue levels exceeded the maximum
limits in only a very few cases. Somerfield's protestations were pointless;
Friends of the Earth had won the PR battle. Realizing that British public
opinion had reset the safety level for pesticides to zero, M&S moved
swiftly to leap ahead of its recalcitrant rivals. Setting aggressive sustainability goals was not just about burnishing the brand or doing the right
thing; it was a way for Marks & Spencer to blindside the competition.

Having launched a couple of quick-hit initiatives to prove M&S
could work with activists and live to tell about it, Barry and a couple
of coconspirators took the next step: win the company's backing for a
bigger, more ambitious battle plan. To make their pitch, they objectively
mapped M&S's performance against sixteen social and environmental
challenges to the company's food business—animal welfare, fair trade,
pesticides, lead standards, packaging, and more. Just as important, they
benchmarked the competition against those same issues. Then they put
the question to the chief of the company's food business: where do you
want Marks & Spencer to win?

Though the goal was to lead on all sixteen issues in their entirety,
it didn't mean that Marks & Spencer had to achieve a first-in-class
ranking individually. On issues for which stakeholders' expectations ran
high and competitors' performance trended low, such as pesticides and
animal welfare, M&S's food chief agreed to aim for the top slot. In those
categories where the company was merely average, such as fish sourcing,
it set a more realistic goal of becoming a fast follower. Such a mix of

pragmatism and ambition was appropriate for a sprawling conglomerate that coveted the winner's circle but couldn't get into racing shape overnight.

Admittedly, it's tough to build an unconventional venture within a conventional business. Managers who are working flat-out to make their quarterly numbers are likely to regard an exotic, values-driven set of targets—such as increasing the number of fish stocks purchased from sustainable sources—as a nettlesome distraction. Barry and his partners used three tactics to overcome such skepticism.

First, they vividly defined the core issues that mattered most to Marks & Spencer's stakeholders and consumers. Because the task force high-lighted sixteen carefully considered actions and showed how progress would be measured, managers didn't have to infer the future from vague pronouncements about "the mission."

Second, they graphically compared M&S's performance with that of its fiercest rivals, and they underlined where the company was merely middling (or worse). That triggered managers' competitive zeal to achieve more.

Third, winning the backing of Marks & Spencer's food business compelled other operating units (clothing, home furnishings, and so on) to jump into the fray. "The food guys were the first to kick the wall in," recalls Barry. "Six months later, every other part of the business had a similar plan."

Challenge: Reap the reward for operating sustainably.
Solution: Authentically communicate your success and then redouble your efforts.

Even as Marks & Spencer set sustainability targets and began to work toward them, it was a behind-the-scenes effort that went largely unnoticed by the outside world. That changed in late 2005. The brand had drifted into a no-man's-land—a dangerous place to be in the UK's hypercompetitive supermarket industry. Back then, M&S was carrying a lot of the costs of operating sustainably—such as ensuring better compliance management in its supply chain—that its low-price competitors (like Tesco and Wal-Mart) didn't bear. In all, it was spending millions of pounds on meeting higher sustainability standards. But because it hadn't communicated those efforts to consumers, it failed to reap the rewards that would normally accrue to a high-trust brand. Marks & Spencer's chief executive at the time, Stuart Rose,[26] gathered the leaders of the conglomerate's businesses and issued a challenge: create a communication vehicle that would bring the company's sustainability efforts to light.

The result was "Look Behind the Label," an ambitious, twelve-month advertising campaign that told the sustainability story behind everyday Marks & Spencer products. The effort was a resounding success; by early 2007, British shoppers voted M&S the country's "greenest supermarket" and deemed it the company "that best looked after its employees."[27] But for Marks & Spencer's strategists, the biggest reward was confirmation that by leading on sustainability issues, the company was redefining its competitive landscape.

M&S's ascension to the top of the eco-heap propelled the big-volume value players to slap back. Tesco, for example, launched a high-profile campaign to declare that it would reduce waste, conserve energy, and put carbon-footprint data labels on all its products. A new battle had been very publicly joined, and it was no longer simply about building the brand or scoring PR points. It was about leveraging sustainability to win market share.

"The big guys wanted their space back," exclaims Barry. "We realized we were really on to something. We're never going to beat them on price. But if we can drag them on to a battlefield that's marked out in terms of trust and responsibility, we've got a chance of winning."

Spurred by the CEO's warning that "complacency kills," Marks & Spencer doubled down on its sustainability bets. Led by Barry, a task force brainstormed more than two hundred social and environmental issues that confronted the company; with a healthy investment of sweat equity, the group eventually narrowed the list to one hundred challenges across five categories: climate change, waste, raw materials, fair trade, and people. The targets were set with an eye toward putting Marks & Spencer ahead of its rivals, but not *too* far ahead.

"We're a mass-market business, and we've got to stay relevant," says Barry. "You want to be demonstrably better than your competitors, but you don't want to look like an outlandish freak."

After running the list through a series of reality checks, Marks & Spencer's senior management committed to fulfilling all one hundred challenges by 2012. Those estimable targets—which span everything from supporting the communities where M&S trades to tripling its sales of organic food, from taking care of employees to fighting climate change—embrace an almost incomprehensible range of activities. Could such a sprawling set of targets signal that Marks & Spencer can't decide what to focus on?

Mike Barry argues otherwise. He insists that the century mark is a "small number" for a company that counts 1.7 million workers in its supply chain, and serves 21 million customers who consume 350 million items of clothing and 2 billion items of food every year. The days of attempting to build a halo around a brand by cherry-picking a single worthy issue, such as organic food—while ignoring all the other social and environmental consequences of a company's actions—are over. Given the accelerating rate of climate change, worldwide water shortages, an epidemic of childhood obesity, and the scores of other challenges confronting global enterprises, incrementalism is insufficient. Marks & Spencer's one hundred commitments announce that the company intends to act systemically and holistically.

Challenge: Communicating the strategy.
Solution: Keep it simple. Say what you mean and do what you say.

People don't support what they can't explain. So it goes with the "corporate social responsibility" tag. Although the label pops up in Mike Barry's title, he's always had some disquiet about it. The words are too technical and too broad. "Even people in the industry interpret them differently," he exclaims.

So in 2007, when it came time to put a name to its one hundred social and environmental targets, Marks & Spencer unveiled not a CSR plan but a Plan A ("because there is no Plan B"). The program's compact title delivers a dramatic sense of urgency. People get it; simplicity matters. The senior team that oversees Plan A is called the How We Do Business (HWDB) committee. There's no "convoluted code," as *The Economist* once asserted, for Marks & Spencer's efforts to do good.[28] The message is unbending; the implication is unambiguous: "how we do business" signals that Plan A is stitched into every part of the enterprise.

Marks & Spencer's point man for Plan A—the executive who must spearhead the company's efforts to attain its goals—is the company's former construction director, Richard Gillies. He's not your typical do-gooder. Having once overseen more than three hundred employees and a budget of £1.4 billion, he seems more at home with spreadsheets and blueprints than with values statements and mission agendas. He mockingly calls CSR "corporate *socialist* responsibility" and dubs environmentalists "the bunny brigade." But having worked at M&S for more than twenty-five years, he is well positioned to corral resources, cajole skeptics, mentor the mediocre, and drive the company toward its Plan A objectives. He makes a powerful case that Plan A is vitally necessary for not only building the company's resiliency but also fulfilling that basic human instinct to contribute to the greater good.

"I've spent my career at Marks & Spencer trying to get people to buy things," says Gillies. "But there's a real desire to do more. When you're on your deathbed and you look back at your life, you want to be able to point to something. You want to be able to say that you helped change your industry."

Challenge: To get everyone on board and hold people accountable.
Solution: Go public with your commitments.

Given the frequency, over the past few years, with which activist groups and bloggers have (often correctly) hurled the greenwashing epithet at big companies, more than a few of these organizations are unwilling to put the spotlight on their social and environmental initiatives. Green business commentators such as Joel Makower, a widely respected writer and consultant on sustainable business issues, opine that the fear of being branded with the "G-word" has caused many companies to "clam up" and forgo the "reputational benefits" that green efforts often convey.[29]

Perhaps this is a wise choice. As we will show in Chapter Five, in which we take an inside look at Nike, the rewards are compelling when companies put their sustainability lens on innovation rather than reputation. But for those "confused and conflicted" companies that Makower cites—anonymous outfits that are "unwilling to talk about what they're doing right"—we can't help but wonder: how can anyone working inside those companies take their efforts seriously, when no one on the outside can hold them accountable?

Marks & Spencer has taken a radically different tack. The most obvious evidence: the Plan A updates that are emblazoned across the electronic ticker in the lobby of the company's headquarters. No doubt, Plan A's conspicuous profile aims to embellish the company's do-good credentials. As former CEO Rose told the *Sunday Times (London)*, "We gain a commercial benefit if we can differentiate ourselves by being genuinely greener."[30] But the program's prominence also serves another function. People notice. And there will be hell to pay if the company doesn't deliver on its commitments. "If we fail," observes Gillies, "it will be a very public failure."

The reason why many big companies find it difficult to execute against "the mission" is that typically, just a small corporate crèche is responsible for it. Realizing this, Marks & Spencer has taken four bold steps to ensure that the majority of its seventy-five thousand employees are accountable for at least a part of Plan A.

1. *Build a glass house.* Transparency builds accountability. The Plan A updates that roll across Marks & Spencer's ticker strip away the opacity that veils so many big organizations; they also put associates and suppliers on notice that the world is following their progress (or lack thereof).

M&S's annual How We Do Business report serves a similar function, with greater depth.

Avoiding the kind of techno-jargon that often plagues the typical CR report, the How We Do Business committee issues detailed, clear-eyed accounts of the company's performance against each of its Plan A targets. It presents unblinking evidence of where progress has stalled—in the summer of 2007, for example, the plan to use biodiesel to fuel the company's trucks backfired when the alternative fuel was shown to be less green than it seemed. The program also enlists an independent auditor, Ernst & Young LLP, to verify that the data is real. And it holds senior management to a very personal accounting by publishing the names of those executives who are responsible for Plan A outcomes. "If you do well, you get a 'well done' from the chief executive," sums up Barry. "If you do badly, you get the knife."

2. *Measure up.* To ensure that it hits its one hundred goals by 2012, M&S has set scores of internal milestones and deadlines for achieving them, such as increasing the percentage of fish stocks from sustainable sources and reducing the number of overtime and safety infractions at its contract factories. Every Plan A target is assigned a delivery manager, whose performance goals are tied to making progress toward the program's objectives. Gillies oversees a color-coded dashboard, dubbed "the Eliminator," which signals whether the Plan A delivery managers are on pace to nail their deadlines.

Each month, the How We Do Business committee reviews the company's Plan A performance, and the executives responsible for the program's pillar categories (climate change, waste, sustainable raw materials, trade partner, and health) are held to account. The purpose of the How We Do Business meetings is to tell it like it is—and make it better. They are very much carrot-and-stick affairs.

So, for example, one of Plan A's most ambitious targets is to achieve zero waste sent to landfills from its six hundred stores, twenty warehouses, and five offices operating in the UK and Ireland. It's an extraordinarily complex challenge, and for several months in late 2008, the team responsible for the target stumbled badly and got a "glowing red" on the Eliminator dashboard, recalls Barry. "The director for that area was hauled before the board and given a very public bollocking. But he was also given additional head count, budget, and technical support to put it right." It's through this mix of metrics, meetings, and tough-love management that Marks & Spencer begins to push Plan A through its org chart and make the mission tangible to everyone in the company.

3. *Get granular.* Although the breadth of Plan A's ambition is undeniably compelling, real progress depends on digging deep into dull-as-dirt details. As Thomas Friedman wryly proclaimed in *Hot, Flat, and Crowded,* "If it isn't boring, it isn't green."[31] So it goes with Marks & Spencer.

To move the needle toward the daunting goal of going carbon neutral, Gillies and his team plumbed the vastly detailed design specifications for the retailer's stores. They found that the weight loadings for the first floors were still based on a time when stock was kept in the top floors. But stock is now stored in warehouses, so the bottom floors no longer need to carry big loads. Lighter floors required less concrete—a major source of carbon dioxide emissions, which contribute to global climate change.[32] "Because we reached way down into some spec document," said Gillies, "we got rid of quite a lot of embedded carbon." It's this kind of painstaking scrutiny, continually replicated in every quarter of the company, that yields dramatic results.

4. *Recruit allies.* Realizing that it can't attain its Plan A goals without getting many more minds into the mix, Marks & Spencer has endeavored to attract thousands of accomplices to its cause.

First, it trained and placed a Plan A "champion" in each of its six hundred stores—Type A advocates who give management a real-world reality check on what works (and more important, what doesn't) and rally their front-line colleagues. So, for example, M&S recycles and reuses two hundred million coat hangers a year—and realizes nearly £8 million in annual savings—largely because its Plan A champions coax their sixty-five thousand colleagues into executing on the edict.

Second, M&S launched a supplier exchange Web site, which allows its two thousand suppliers in thirty countries to contribute feedback and best-practice ideas for advancing Plan A's commitments. It's basically a forum in which needs and solutions can find each other. So when M&S sought to cut the polymer content in its dry-cleaning bags, a Sri Lankan supplier discovered that the bags' thickness could be reduced by 50 percent without weakening their durability.

Third, the company continues to regularly reach out to NGOs. It partnered with Oxfam to create a clothes exchange that diverted fourteen hundred tons of used clothing from landfills and raised £1.8 million for charity. To lure consumers to donate clothes to Oxfam, M&S awarded them £5 vouchers that are redeemable when they spend £35 or more—an amount that's above the retailer's average purchase price for clothing. Essentially, the vouchers are an incentive to spend. Marks & Spencer gets a "bigger basket" on clothing purchases, Oxfam gets a new source of revenue, and consumers get a discount. Once again, the adage proves true: business *can* do well by doing good.

AN AGENDA FOR BUILDING MISSION-DRIVEN COMPANIES

With Plan A, improving the environment and contributing to society are the goals. Building the brand and boosting the bottom line are the great by-products. So it was that in early 2009 Marks & Spencer reported that Plan A, which needed an initial outlay of £200 million, was cost-neutral—that is, the program had generated enough savings to offset the investments it required. In the years ahead, Marks & Spencer expects the program to generate some fairly significant profits. A worsening economy or the multiple blows from a pack of aggressive competitors might well dash those expectations. But even if they do, Marks & Spencer has crafted a compelling blueprint for big companies that genuinely want to adopt a bold mission:

- Work with your critics—their diversity might spur your creativity.
- Think competitively. The mission is not a feel-good strategy. It's a battle plan.
- Commit to an audacious goal—one that's big enough to inspire people to do more.

- Define targets, set deadlines. Progress will come only when people are clear about what comes next.
- Billboard your values and your goals. The prospect of a very public hanging will spur urgency and action.
- Conduct a series of continual companywide—and communitywide—conversations. Eliciting many ideas increases the likelihood that a few good ideas will emerge.
- To advance the mission, recruit mission champions.

By following these design specs, even an established company can reimagine its true purpose and thereby create products and services that stakeholders and consumers regard as truly extraordinary.

————————

By definition, every truly responsible revolutionary embraces a set of principles that are worth championing and a core purpose that's worth serving. Organic Valley and Marks & Spencer, two vastly different organizations, show that by building a unique sense of purpose, you not only begin to achieve high performance thresholds, you also rally associates, consumers, and stakeholders to your cause. A company's mission, it turns out, really does matter. And if the mission is truly compelling, it fuels a sense of destiny that's urgent enough to overcome the pull of the past—and meaningful enough to make a difference in the world.

NOT A COMPANY, BUT A COMMUNITY

A BLUEPRINT FOR SUMMONING PEOPLE'S POTENTIAL

In May 2008, at his last shareholders' meeting as the chairman of Southwest Airlines, Herb Kelleher wept when he spoke about how much he cared about the company's employees. It wasn't an act.[1]

For most of the past two decades, Southwest has been one of the few bright stars in the airline industry's gloomy firmament—the one high-flier that, until the brutal 2008–2009 recession,[2] was profitable year in and year out, even when so many of the legacy airlines struggled for survival. As far as the Kool-smoking, Wild Turkey–sipping cofounder of Southwest was concerned, the key to the company's enduring achievement lay in the indomitable performance of its employees. By putting its people on a par with its customers and ahead of its investors, Southwest has summoned more than enough resilience and tenacity to lower costs, drive revenue, outperform its rivals, and fulfill its core mission: to bring the "freedom to fly" to people who otherwise could afford only to drive.

"When you treat [your employees] right, they will treat your customers right," Kelleher once told Fortune. "That has been a powerful competitive weapon for us."[3]

Kelleher's insight underlines the notion that building a purpose-driven company—or, as Southwest puts it, a "company with a conscience"—starts on the inside, with employees, and not on the outside, with green-product launches and do-good, cause-related marketing campaigns. Yet can that be the whole reason why Southwest is so often in the black and always advancing its mission? Can the secret to a big, complicated company's success really be so easily explained? The answer is yes—and no.

The ultimate performance test of any company is not how fast it can grow over the next few quarters, but how consistently it can grow over years and decades. The ultimate "responsibility" test of any company is not how cleverly it can craft its mission statement, but how deeply it can instill its values and vision into the hearts and minds of its employees. In a world where change is constant, such a challenge demands the full spirit and will of every associate.

When a company isn't as innovative with its people as it is with setting strategy and developing products, it won't be innovative over the long run. Herb Kelleher's simple maxim cuts to the heart of the matter: people are the key to enduring, superior performance. As one of the architects of a long-ago (but still relevant) McKinsey study on the competition for talent once put it, "Talented people, in the right kind of culture, have better ideas, execute those ideas better, and even develop other people better."[4] Yet "treating your employees like your customers" doesn't begin to describe the challenge of creating a workplace that leverages all the creativity and initiative that people have to offer. For all of the thousands of companies that have proclaimed themselves to be stellar corporate citizens, far too many have failed to meet the minimum requirement that they fully engage associate's hearts and minds.[5]

In 2008, the consulting company Towers Perrin conducted an ambitious survey of ninety thousand employees in large and medium-sized companies across eighteen countries.[6] The study's overarching goal was to measure the degree to which people feel committed to their work. Even for those who are jaded by the apathy that pervades many big companies, the results were eye-opening: 71 percent of the respondents said they were "disengaged" or "disenchanted" at work. The study reported that employees "care a lot about their work" and they want to "learn and grow." However, the unvarnished survey results revealed that, sadly, companies aren't just wasting people's skill and knowledge—their stultifying cultures actively discourage people from contributing more, even though most employees say they are keen to do so.

The survey's findings are especially sobering for any company that seeks to contribute to society, for society's foremost expectation of a good company is that it creates a great workplace.

For responsible companies, creating an exceptional work environment is both an imperative and a sign of progress. According to a 2007 national opinion poll conducted by the public relations firm Fleishman-Hillard and the National Consumers League,[7] 40 percent of Americans believe that the most important proof of stellar corporate citizenship—even more than environmental stewardship and philanthropy—is a proven track record of supporting communities and treating employees well. That's a necessary first step, but it's not nearly enough to create the dynamic, inclusive environment that frees people to give their all.

The lesson for leaders: to galvanize people so they deliver their very best every day, responsible companies must build a culture that acts more like a community than the typical corporate hierarchy—a community in which profits fuel the drive to fulfill a larger purpose.

Few observers have better summed up the power of the community model than Gary Hamel, the author and business strategist. In his book *The Future of Management* (written with this book's coauthor, Bill Breen), Hamel argued that communities excel at "inspiring people to go above and beyond. When it comes to mobilizing human capability, communities outperform bureaucracies."[8] In a workplace that operates like a community, people are propelled by a cause that's bigger than "to increase shareholder value." It's a place where people are bound by a shared vision—where the answer to "What's in it for *me*?" depends entirely on "what *we* can accomplish." It's a place that relies a whole lot less on "orders" and a whole lot more on "offers"—where people want to go the extra mile because they have the chance to offer their time and talent to projects of their own choosing.

Above all, the company that works like a community is a place where people have enough autonomy to make critical decisions, with the expectation that they are responsible for the results. But how do you make that happen? How do you get around the obstacles and communicate the risks that come with hierarchies? How do you launch low-cost, less-risky experiments in community building? How do you then learn from the results and begin to create cultures in which people are absolutely amped to do the work that ultimately improves the bottom line and makes a difference in the world? You can start by meeting a company that's confronting the challenges of building community-based alternatives to corporate hierarchies—and that's yielding some startling results.

TO BREAK THE BUREAUCRATIC HIERARCHY: LINDEN LAB

What does it feel like to be "managed" in a conventional corporate setting? Julian Birkinshaw, a professor of strategic management at the London Business School, posed just this question in a 2008 article.[9] He proposed that leaders would benefit by looking at the corporate world through the eyes of those who must follow. If they did, they would quickly come to experience that stomach-churning, sweat-inducing emotion that predominates all too many businesses: chronic dread. "Fear is endemic in the workplace," writes Birkinshaw. "We worry about looking foolish in a meeting, we worry about not living up to expectations, and we are [frightened] that we might lose our job."

A cynic might dismiss fear as the price that must be paid for goosing higher productivity and greater efficiencies out of employees. But fear has a way of boomeranging back on performance. It turns colleagues into conscripts; they'll work diligently, but rarely willingly. And as Hamel observes, an industrious workforce almost never outperforms an enthusiastic workforce.

In fact, it's now documented that fear also tamps down day-to-day innovation in the workplace. In a groundbreaking study based on more than twelve thousand daily journal entries of mid-level employees at seven companies, Harvard Business School professor Teresa Amabile found that anger, fear, and anxiety are "negatively associated" with business creativity. "Joy and love," she told *Fast Company* magazine, are creativity's real stimulants. They foster a nourishing environment in which people feel comfortable and confident enough to make the cognitive connections that lead to breakthrough ideas. Concluded Amabile: "One day's happiness often predicts the next day's creativity."[10]

John Mackey, the cofounder and CEO of Whole Foods Market, likewise understands that fear won't elicit extraordinary contributions from people or inspire them to summon all of their energy and imagination at work every day. In 1992, a year after he took Whole Foods public, Mackey recommitted himself to the challenge of "creating an organization based on love instead of fear."[11] You might think that Whole Foods' market cap, which has climbed to more than $44 billion in the nearly two decades since the company's IPO—despite a drop during the 2008–2009 recession—would inspire others to follow Mackey's lead. But all too often, executives who've scrambled over the backs of colleagues on their way to summiting the corporate pyramid interpret "big-hearted" as "soft-headed." For these skeptics, loving your employees is an imperative that's more often heralded than heeded.

Nevertheless, it *is* possible to come across workplaces that are organizing around openhearted, community-based virtues like happiness, love, altruism, autonomy, and service. We found one such company a couple of blocks off of the Embarcadero, near San Francisco's waterfront. Linden Lab is a digital media outfit that's best known for its chief creation, an online, virtual-reality environment called Second Life, whose name is synonymous with its promise: to give its users (or "residents") the chance to build a whole new, alternative existence—in other words, a second life.[12]

Philip Rosedale, Linden's charismatic founder and chairman, took one long night to build a simple but potent tool for stifling workplace fear. He calls it the "Love Machine." It's a Web page that lets any of Linden's roughly three hundred associates zap a quick-hit message of appreciation to a colleague. Say a coder beats a do-or-die deadline for patching a troublesome bug that's infected Second Life's grid. You click on the Love Machine, write a quick thank-you, and hit Send. In an instant, the bug maven gets a message with a subject line that reads, "Love from [Your Name]." She feels good, because she's received the online equivalent of a long-stemmed rose. And you feel good, because you've "spread the love."

Tossing off a love note is fun and infectious, and on average, every Linden associate—including the 25 percent who work remotely—plies the Love Machine about once a day. Over any given twenty-four-hour period, roughly three hundred such missives wend their way across Linden's intranet—and everyone in the company can watch them flow. Each affectionate dispatch makes a small but positive contribution toward building a collaborative community. The cumulative effect of these daily waves of gratitude is to wash away some of the cynicism and insecurity that plague so many workplaces and to let individual accomplishment and appreciation shine through. This is especially critical for techno-driven environments such as Linden's, where so much of work (and work's rewards) is often intangible.

In today's networked workplace, projects are frequently distributed across teams; work consists mostly of nailing deadlines and staying on budget. The *Wall Street Journal* columnist Jared Sandberg writes, in a piece on the anonymity of the modern workplace, that it's often tough to "find gratification from work that is largely invisible, or from delivering goods that are often metaphorical."[13] Cocooned as we often are in quiet cubicles, it's difficult to see the fruits of individual labor and to define individual success.

Citing research from Homa Bahrami, a senior lecturer at UC Berkeley's Haas School of Business, Sandberg asserts, "Information-age

employees measure their accomplishment in net worth, company reputation, networks of relationships, and the products and services they're
associated with ... " Linden's Love Machine delivers a virtual pat on
the back that isn't filtered through a boss; it's direct and peer-to-peer.
It takes those subjective elements that Bahrami identifies—the relationships and reputation that help people measure their success—and makes
them real. More than that, it makes them empowering.

"In a conventional corporate hierarchy, people are subjected to a
flood of information every day," Rosedale told us. "And the emotional
tone of most of those emails and vmails is negative. That's because much
of management is all about keeping people on track. Which is fine,
except that what you hear is, 'you're late' or 'you didn't fix it.' If most
of your incoming messages are like a series of small clubs pounding away
at you, it's very difficult to do your best work."[14]

The Love Machine, contends Rosedale, takes the internal
messaging that flows through most corporations and replaces its familiar
and expected negativity with something that's far more affirming and
potentially more effective. Praising people for a job well done boosts
their self-esteem, makes their work visible, and increases the odds
that their next contribution will warrant a thank-you instead of a "you
messed up."

Radically, Subversively Responsible

Linden Lab might seem like an unlikely model for any company that
aspires to confront the world's social and environmental challenges.
There's no SVP of Corporate Responsibility on its org chart. The company doesn't bother putting out an annual CR report. And it's doubtful
that you'll ever find a Linden exec keynoting a Business and Sustainability conference. And then there's Linden's Second Life, a vast, richly
pixilated universe that includes a tiered section for cybersex of every
variety ("X-Rated Continent") as well as anatomically immaculate,
buffed, and coiffed denizens (or "avatars") who are tributes to the talent
and self-absorption of their human alter egos—that is, their creators.

But dig a little deeper, and you begin to glimpse Second Life's
magic, which lies in its capacity to give anyone with a fast Internet

connection and an adequate graphics card the power and the tools to create anything that they are driven enough to imagine. Linden Lab supplies the architecture for Second Life, but those in-world residents own what they build. It's their intellectual property; they can claim copyright on it, and they can make money from it. It's this partnership in cocreation that lets Linden Lab begin to live up to its lofty ambition: to create a virtual world that "advances the human condition."

So a part-time artist living in the Boston area can create a big-haired, snaggle-toothed avatar named Filthy Fluno and use it to make a slew of "in-world" friends who buy enough of his real-world art to let him quit his real-life day job.[15] Or a teenager in São Paulo can build a virtual café—an option he'd never have in Brazil—rake in a stack of virtual currency (called "Linden dollars"), convert it into cold, hard *reais*, and pay his family's bills. Then there's the massively paralyzed Japanese man who uses an experimental headset, which monitors his brain waves, to control an avatar and "fly" in Second Life.

Giant multinationals like IBM and Toyota have also moved "in-world," to experiment and collaborate in what amounts to the first iteration of tomorrow's three-dimensional Web. Harvard and M.I.T. are among the many universities that have opened some form of virtual campus in Second Life. The University of California Davis Medical Center, with funding from the Centers for Disease Control, has even created virtual clinics in Second Life to train emergency workers who might be called on to rapidly set up medical facilities in the event of a biological attack or some other national crisis.

"We hear it all the time," says Rosedale. "Second Life is an incredibly powerful change agent that's of real benefit to people."

Second Life's "for-benefit" imperative connects to an equally powerful for-profit model. It makes money mostly by selling and leasing digital real estate, and its capacity to create land is boundless. In the spring of 2009, its in-world population swelled to more than one million residents, a nearly twofold increase over the previous year. Second Life's three-dimensional universe is a magnet for currency speculators, designers, and other entrepreneurs, who sell services and products ranging from digital clothing to body parts, ray guns to real estate to prefab housing. Linden dollars are easily cashed out for real-world credit-card credits, and Second Life's robust virtual economy grew to roughly US$450 million in 2009.

As the aforementioned Love Machine might indicate, Linden Lab's model for building a workplace that feels like a community is almost as peculiar, if not as exotic, as Second Life itself. But breakthrough innovation rarely comes from the mainstream. Linden's approach to community building offers some radical yet practical lessons for surmounting three big risks that are found in far too many corporate hierarchies.

Hierarchical Risk #1: In a hierarchy, the lion's share of recognition and recompense goes to the self-promoters and those who hold the biggest titles. The real heroes are left unsung, which suppresses people's spirit and will—why work harder and risk more, they reason, when those who are most deserving go unrewarded? *Linden's Remedy:* The community—not some select group of corporate overlords—does the rewarding.

Recognition is a fertilizer for ambition. When you are publicly acknowledged for going beyond the call of duty and you're compensated with a bonus—the corporate equivalent of hazardous duty pay—it's unlikely that you'll shy away from the next big battle. So it's astonishing that so many companies rely on a clubby group of executives to dispense bonuses, which too often go to the usual suspects—the favored and the politically connected, usually in sales or senior management. Linden Lab takes the power to reward away from the clique and their claque and gives it to the people. It does this through another software tool, called the Rewarder.

Each quarter, every associate is given an equal share of a portion of Linden's net profit—recently, about one thousand dollars per person. The money comes with one stipulation: you cannot keep it for yourself. You must click on the Rewarder and use it to redistribute your share to those whom you believe did the most to help the company over the past three months. You can send the total to one overachiever or divide it among several. It's your call.

The Rewarder's two-year history shows that, by and large, it does a superior job of fairly recognizing performance. No doubt a few may abuse the system and patronize their friends. But most people tend to do the right thing, because the Rewarder empowers them to steer the company in the right direction. "If you want this company to succeed," says Rosedale, "you'll give the money away in a rational manner."

The Rewarder takes one of the more politically fraught calls that any company must make—deciding with whom to share the spoils of its success—and invites the entire community to decide. It defuses the problem by decentralizing it.

The Rewarder also tallies each person's bonus allocation. When Linden's senior management looks at the top ten recipients in any given quarter, roughly half the winners are unsurprising—they're Linden's consistently best performers, and they are known to all. Sprinkled among them, however, are people whom Linden's leaders might think are unremarkable, but according to the community, are exceptional. The Rewarder puts the spotlight on unsung heroes—those innovative, driven souls who deliver the goods but aren't particularly adept at advertising their accomplishments. They are publicly acclaimed and their standard compensation is boosted by their peers, which gives Linden a better chance of holding on to them—and a better shot at keeping the community healthy.

Hierarchical Risk #2: The big dogs at the sharp end of the pyramid wield the annual performance review as a way to preserve their power advantage.
Linden's Remedy: Invite the community to review the big dogs.

It's an almost universal truth that every corporation conducts an annual performance review, and just about everyone hates it. Performance reviews are supposed to take a fair-minded look at associates' work, pinpoint where they can improve, and help determine their pay. But almost invariably, reviews are one-sided, boss-to-minion monologues whose claims to objectivity are absurd. Samuel Culbert, a professor at the UCLA Anderson School of Management, is one among many critics who sees little value in the traditional approach to evaluating people. "[A] boss-administered review is little more than a dysfunctional pretense," writes Culbert. "It's a negative to corporate performance, an obstacle to straight-talk relationships, and a prime cause of low morale at work."[16]

Linden Lab also uses performance reviews, but it breaks the corporate mold by inviting the entire community to weigh in, via the Love Machine. Every three months, people pick the ten Love Notes that they think best capture their major contributions over the previous quarter. Those notes, which are essentially merit badges awarded by the community, go into everyone's reviews, which are published on an internal Web site for all other employees to see. In a sense, the company conducts a community-wide review of each person's most recent contributions, recognizes individual achievement, and holds people accountable for their performance.

What's more, Linden has worked to ensure that the community's "straight talk" flows vertically as well as horizontally. One example: each quarter, when he was the CEO, Rosedale would use SurveyMonkey.com to send out a quick questionnaire to everyone in the company. He posed three questions:

1. "Do you want to keep me or find a new CEO?"
2. "Over the last three months, did I get better at this job or worse?"
3. "Why?"

The voting was completely anonymous, so people felt protected enough to deliver frank feedback, and Rosedale shared the results from those first two questions with Linden's entire community. He kept the responses to that third question to himself; almost invariably, people's comments were uncompromising and plenty powerful.

"You can argue with a mentor, but you can't argue with the crowd," Rosedale concedes. "When every third person says, 'You're too scattered,' it's the truth. These decentralized voting systems are authoritative."

The overall feedback was consistently and overwhelmingly positive, because Rosedale is generally perceived to be an inspirational founder. But he could see a trend line developing—there would come a time when the majority of the community would conclude that although he wasn't doing a "worse" job, it was becoming increasingly difficult for him to improve. The community-wide survey wasn't the determining factor in Rosedale's decision to launch a very public search and tap Mark Kingdon, the CEO of the interactive marketing company Organic, as Linden's new chief executive in March 2008. But the community's collective voice helped shape Rosedale's thinking. "You project a point in the future where you're going to need to leave," he says. "And that's pretty cool."

Skeptics might insist that other companies also encourage two-way conversations between leaders and followers, through multisource assessment mechanisms like 360-degree reviews. But Linden is aiming for something bigger. By using tools like the CEO Survey, the Rewarder, and the Love Machine, Linden eschews the top-down monologues that typify corporate hierarchies. Instead, it plays host to an ongoing, community-wide dialogue, which ranges from who is valued at any given moment, to who the unheralded superstars are, to whether the leaders are leading effectively, and much, much more. When individuals feel they have a voice—when the conversation flows from the bottom up as well as from the top down—they forge deeper connections to the community. And those connections drive execution.

"I suspect that in the future, hierarchical organizations will increasingly work like democracies, where today's executives become more like senators," says Rosedale. "Their job will be to provoke conversations and provide strategic guidance. There'll be a high degree of transparency, and if the leaders aren't leading effectively, the community will vote them out and elect a new team."

Hierarchical Risk #3: Managers define and assign tasks, with little or no input from those who must do the work.
Linden's Remedy: Give people the freedom to design their own jobs.

As Hamel asserts in *The Future of Management,* in a hierarchy, people give their diligence and, ideally, their intellect to projects that are assigned to them. In a community, people volunteer their higher-order capabilities—passion and creativity—to projects of their own choosing. Communities evoke bigger contributions from people because they offer rewards that are more emotional than financial: the chance to do the work that matters most to the worker, not the manager. Linden understands this.

In its first years as a start-up, instead of assigning engineers to work on a specific project, Linden let them choose their work from a vast database of tasks. That way, teams formed organically, not coercively, based on people's shared interests. Rosedale believes that by letting people set their own strategic direction, they think less like employees and more like entrepreneurs. In an interview with *Inc.* magazine, he recalled how early on, Linden was organized around one fundamental rule: "Tell everybody in an email every week what you are doing, then make some progress and tell everybody in an email how you did it."[17] That way, the pressure to perform comes not from bosses, but from peers—a far more powerful group of motivators.

As Linden's headcount grew to more than three hundred people, Rosedale's "organizational scheme" evolved. It still operates around the notion that individuals should be free enough to choose their projects, so long as the community holds them accountable for the results. But Linden's principle of self-selected commitment is now more focused. People no longer email their weekly to-do lists; they now use a self-reporting tool called "A&Os" (achievements and objectives), where they share with the company what they accomplished the previous week and what they will work on in the upcoming week. Because the A&Os are completely transparent, everyone has a high degree of peripheral vision, so they see what others are working on and weigh in with comments and ideas. In this way, Linden yokes the collective wisdom of the entire organization and brings it to bear on decisions large (hiring Mark Kingdon) and small (naming conference rooms).

What's changed, largely through Kingdon's prodding, is that people are no longer *completely* free to follow their curiosity and pick their own projects. Sometimes, work is assigned to them. Linden now uses a small, multidisciplinary team to identify the company's biggest initiatives, then either designates or invites people to contribute. In this way, Linden is attempting to corral people's capacity for innovation without dampening their initiative. "We're moving from the House of Yes, where you can work on whatever you like, to the House of Reason, where you work on what makes the most strategic sense," Kingdon told us.

Kingdon continues to push the community to constantly talk, every day, about the company's direction—and thereby influence it. Linden taps the community's opinion through the Rewarder, which allows associates to allocate points to those projects that they believe will most benefit the company and are therefore most deserving of the company's resources. Each point has a value that's based on the company's quarterly performance, and those who contribute to successfully completed projects receive a bonus based on the point total. Essentially, the Rewarder disperses decision making across the entire organization, by giving everyone a voice in setting strategy. And it provokes people to take an entrepreneurial approach to their work.

"We're taking the dynamics of the marketplace and applying it to decision making," says Rosedale. "This approach is highly transparent and very aggressive. Because it rewards risk, it pushes people to come together, attack a problem, solve it, and move on."

Lessons from Linden

What can we take away from Linden's bold approach to building a workplace that functions like a purpose-driven community? Let us suggest three critical lessons.

One: Transparency fuels accountability.

Just as transparency forces companies to respond to their stakeholders, it prompts individual associates to answer to their peers. When Lindenites post their weekly objectives and their achievements, they're visible to the entire organization. People know, with crystal clarity, who's stumbling and who's coming through. Linden strives for the same high degree of transparency that you'd find on a basketball court. Even as you're racing down-court, you can see, out of the corner of your eye, how your teammates are doing. You know who's open and who needs help. And everybody knows the score.

Two: Purpose matters.

When a company's self-conception doesn't extend much beyond its financial objectives, it more than likely won't stretch people's ambition and drive. What's needed is a lofty sense of purpose. Linden Lab thinks of itself not as a company but as a community of people working to "advance the human condition." This vision animates everything it does and inspires a concerted effort to do more.

Three: Let them decide.

Transparency ensures that there are no "nobodies" at Linden Lab; because people's contributions are completely visible, everybody is a "somebody." Accountability for specific deliverables drives people to deliver at least as much value as their peers do. And a big, inspiring purpose keeps Linden pointed toward True North.

Once those three attributes are in place, decision making can be decentralized and pushed to the front lines, where it will have the greatest impact. That might look strange when judged according to conventional, command-and-control corporate practice. Or does it? Consider Rosedale's pick for the ultimate decentralized organization: the U.S. Army.

"The Army instills in you some principles that you'll hopefully live by, and makes clear that you're responsible for the results of your actions," Rosedale asserts. "But once the shooting starts, you make your own decisions. You don't ask permission to return fire. And that's what we're trying to do with these highly decentralized systems. Build in that transparency and accountability, and then get out of people's way. Far more often than not, they'll make the best choices."

Building the "people part" of a responsible company doesn't mean you've got to turn the place into a commune. Rosedale is the furthest thing from a blissed-out Utopian—he knows it would be impossible to get folks to show up for work every day without the promise of a paycheck. "I'm an entrepreneur, and I've had to make money from the time I was seventeen," he says. "I definitely believed from the get-go that this was a great business opportunity—a tremendous moneymaker."

But Rosedale was hungry to combine the profit motive with the innovation motive—to create a virtual world where people can free their imaginations, and to create a workplace that replaces hierarchy with a bit of humanity and humility. The past can't predict the future, but Linden's ten-year history suggests that modeling the company on a community has already amplified Lindenites' ability to do more. By making the connection between purpose, freedom, accountability, and participative decision-making, Linden stands a better chance of sustaining a resilient, innovative workplace. The folks at Linden would certainly understand Herb Kelleher's implicit message: give people their wings, and they'll take you to new heights.

THE USER'S GUIDE TO BUILDING A PURPOSE-DRIVEN COMMUNITY: SEVENTH GENERATION

Having dipped into Linden Lab's real-world workplace, perhaps you're persuaded: responsible companies that are built on a community model summon from people more zeal, imagination, and resourcefulness than those top-down hierarchies that dominate the business landscape. Maybe you've even imagined, through Linden's example, how you might launch some low-cost, community-building experiments in your organization. But then, reality intrudes.

You're not the chief executive of a company the size of Southwest Airlines, where you can upend the place's conventions with one quick decree. And you haven't launched an outfit like a Linden Lab, where you're free to experiment with market-based decision making and democratic design. Resources are tight, and you lack the clout to create even an off-the-books initiative. Or perhaps you're so good at your current work, senior management would never let you take on an initiative as amorphous-sounding as "reimagining the workplace." Besides, you're just one person. How much can you do? As it turns out, quite a bit.

The creation of easy-to-adapt mechanisms like the Love Machine and the Rewarder deliver valuable, proof-of-concept lessons for any responsible organization that wants to take a revolutionary leap toward building a purpose-driven community. But don't think you need a fiat from the founder to agitate for change. Just consider the example of Susan Johnson, Seventh Generation's former director of western sales. She seized on one of the fundamental principles of any community-based organization—the freedom to determine her own destiny—to create a whole new career for herself and a whole new opportunity for the company. During its inception, her change effort required neither money nor sign-off, yet it sparked a cultural shift that continues to unfold in our Burlington, Vermont, headquarters.

Having joined Seventh Generation in 1999, after a six-year stint at Tom's of Maine, Johnson was responsible for all accounts west of the Mississippi—in all, about five thousand stores and co-ops. Although her territory was vast, her sales force was small and her marketing funds limited. Especially in the first years of this decade, Seventh Generation relied on sales brokers to represent the brand in individual stores and sell our lines of green home care and personal-care products like laundry detergent, dishwashing soap, diapers, recycled paper towels, and feminine-care items. These brokers were our "feet on the ground," but they weren't ours exclusively; they'd typically handle as many as forty other natural brands such as Stonyfield Farms and Tom's of Maine.

Admittedly, it was a tough challenge: Johnson (and our other sales managers) had to nail quarterly targets, but it was the brokers who handled our immediate sales. If they didn't hit their numbers, Johnson wouldn't hit hers. To succeed, she had to ensure that the brokers could intelligently and passionately discuss the details of our products' features, benefits, and points of difference with store managers and buyers. Essentially, she had to turn the brokers into knowledgeable, effective advocates for the Seventh Generation brand—which meant that she spent as much time educating as selling.

Johnson's talent for coaching brokers helped make her our top sales manager, but it took a meeting with Whole Foods Market, our largest customer, to show that a more ambitious approach to education could dramatically impact Seventh Generation's relationships with key stakeholders.

If you've ever shopped at Whole Foods, you know that its stores are stuffed full of gorgeously arrayed organic and natural food products. Their allure was so powerful that ironically, it caused a problem for some Whole Foods emporiums: the vast majority of shoppers wheeled their carts around the stores' perimeters, with their colorful displays of glistening produce and luscious cheeses and meats. But comparatively few shoppers dipped into the center of the store, where paper towels, diapers, and cleaning products from Seventh Generation and other brands were displayed, sometimes in ho-hum uniformity. Sales were so anemic in some categories that industry insiders took to calling the center aisles "the prison."

In early 2006, Johnson, along with three other Seventh Generation executives, found herself standing before an audience composed of nearly every Whole Foods grocery-team leader in northern California. Her task: to introduce them to Seventh Generation, so they could move more product. She did more than that. For sixty minutes, she and our other execs talked about the rising incidence of asthma and chemical sensitivity cases due to indoor air pollution, and a growing desire among consumers to create healthy homes. Johnson, in particular, delivered stories and statistics showing that an increasing number of consumers were purchasing their chlorine-free diapers and natural cleaning products from grocery stores, not from Whole Foods. She fired up the team leaders' competitive juices and gave them the ammunition to advocate not just for the Seventh Generation brand, but also for the entire "Living Home" sector. Recalls Johnson: "I had to build the category before I could build our business."

For the Whole Foods folks who were listening that day, suddenly the proverbial lightbulb flashed on. They could see how natural home-care products aligned seamlessly with their natural food products. They understood why it didn't make sense for consumers to buy organic produce and then prepare meals on countertops cleaned with chemicals. Soon we were collaborating with Whole Foods on developing promotions and auxiliary displays, and we were educating store personnel so they could articulate our benefits and motivate shoppers to get into those center aisles.

As a result, Seventh Generation's sales at Whole Foods quickly improved, and Johnson soon found herself having a revelation of her own. She was burned out on all the travel that came with selling. She was ready to invent a new role for herself, one in which she would build educational initiatives that would turn not just brokers but many other stakeholders into advocates for the "healthy, living home" and for Seventh Generation. To her mind, her goals and the company's needs were completely compatible. But she knew that getting the buy-in from senior management would be a very hard sell. She was the company's most productive sales manager; the very idea of giving up her order book would freak everyone out. Still, she was undeterred.

Johnson's effort to launch a full-blown educational initiative took well over a year. Her story is best understood in terms of how it overcame some of the seemingly intractable management myths that are embraced in so many conventional companies—myths that often snuff the spark that ignites innovation.

Myth #1: Never mess with success.

In 2006, Seventh Generation's annual revenues totaled $64 million, a mere rounding error when compared with Procter & Gamble's $56 billion. Sure, we believed the axiom that you "can't grow the company without growing the people," but we were an underdog competing in an industry of mastiffs. Understandably, senior management was less than thrilled with the notion of letting our top seller abandon her post. Johnson's territory accounted for over 50 percent of our annual sales. If she left to create a position that (at least in the short run) generated zero sales, how would we pick up the slack?

Johnson was smart; she didn't overreach. Her first move was to win a key ally: she outlined her embryonic idea to our VP of sales, John Murphy. Buoyed by the positive results from Whole Foods, Murphy encouraged Johnson to develop her plan further and promised that if senior management pushed back too hard, he would advocate for her—so long as she continued to achieve her sales goals. Murphy's positive response enticed Johnson to pull together a presentation, and in September 2006 she pitched her idea to the senior team. Looking back, three key factors made her case persuasive:

- *Her logic was irrefutable.* Given our limited resources, it was clear we needed to seed teams of evangelists in stores across the country, to spread the news about our products.

- *Her data spoke volumes.* Johnson's research—such as the data point that 90 percent of purchasing decisions are made in the store—demonstrated that if store personnel knew our products and truly believed in their safety and efficacy, they would be our most effective influencers.

- *Her idea dovetailed with the company's purpose.* A big part of Seventh Generation's mission is to help shoppers become conscious consumers. Johnson's initiative had the potential to educate people at the point of sale, where our message would have the biggest impact.

Johnson's pitch looked promising. Even so, some on the executive team had a hard time justifying paying her a sales director's salary for teaching store clerks. So we struck a compromise. Johnson could pull together a trial program and give it a road test. But until she proved that it would work, she'd have to keep selling.

Myth #2: Radical means risky.

It might have been unduly risky to let one of our top earners devote a good chunk of her time to an initiative that could easily have gone nowhere. After all, time is a nonrenewable resource, and especially back then, our resources were tightly constrained. But we balanced the risk by keeping Johnson on her day job and investing just enough in funding and additional talent to test her hypothesis. A radical test doesn't have to be expensive. And this experiment, even if it blew up, would not have brought the company down.

Although this was far from a bet-the-company move, Johnson's project did begin to bend Seventh Generation's culture. She had already injected the notion that it was at least plausible, even for someone at her senior-level pay grade, to follow her instincts and blaze a new career. What's more, she gave people the chance to volunteer part of their time to work on an off-budget project that just might become the cornerstone of a more community-based culture.

Google is famous for its "20-percent time"—its license for developers to devote one-fifth of their work to any project that kindles their curiosity. With Johnson's education initiative, we followed Google's lead and gave her the green light to recruit a cross-functional "pursuit" team of six volunteers. Like Johnson, they'd still have to hold down their day jobs, even as they pitched into this new opportunity. Essentially, these enterprising folks—who came from customer service, R&D, marketing, and other departments—gave "120-percent time." Animated by the prospect of helping to do the work that makes for a more conscious consumer, they believed the experience they gleaned would help them in their own day-to-day work. And no doubt they hungered for the psychic reward of putting their talent behind a project that truly mattered to them.

The team's first step was to benchmark other companies that had innovated around education. So they watched Starbucks work to continually upgrade its baristas' skills, and they learned that educating is not just a one-time event. They hung out with an Ekin ("Nike" spelled backward), who drops into sporting-goods stores and shows salespeople how Nike shoes are made and highlights their performance attributes. They saw how Patagonia inspires and informs people through its stirring catalogue and online essays. And they sat in with chefs from Spectrum Organics, the makers of artisan-crafted specialty oils like toasted hazelnut and pumpkin seed, who prepared sumptuous meals for Whole Foods associates—they "experienced" Spectrum by consuming its products. Sums up Johnson: "We learned that story and experience can influence people so much more powerfully than facts."

By the end of their benchmarking sessions, the team had come up with a title for their campaign: "Influence the Influencer." But as they soon discovered, the first idea isn't always the best idea.

OVERCOMING HIERARCHY, BUILDING COMMUNITY: PATAGONIA

Hierarchical Risk: A soul-sapping focus on managing people's time.

Patagonia's Remedy: Recognize that time is a nonrenewable resource—let people husband and manage it themselves.

Patagonia, the outdoor-apparel company and a green-business pioneer, is well known for creating a work culture that's both demanding and humane. Discretionary time is the primary fuel that power's Patagonia's performance.

Patagonia needs to attract alpha adventurers to its workplace, so it gives people wide latitude for deciding when to work and when to head for the big outdoors. When they're out biking and climbing and skiing, associates are also testing product prototypes and generating fresh insights. Their zeal rubs off on customers, and their insights—however zany—yield ideas. And breakthrough ideas have kept Patagonia ahead of its competitors for more than two decades.

Casey Sheahan, Patagonia's CEO, told us that three times a week, he takes a ninety-minute bike ride up into the hills east of the company's office in Ventura, California. An avid fly fisherman, he often uses the ride to check out a portion of the Ventura River that's a part-time home to steelhead trout. "My original ideas don't come when I'm sitting in this office," he asserts. "They come when I'm out on the bike. My mind clears and suddenly I'm thinking, 'Where are we going next? What's the three-year roadmap going to look like?' The ideas start flooding in—so many that sometimes I've got to pull off to the side of the road and write them down."

The company's founder, Yvon Chouinard—who still slips away for months at a time to climb and ski—argues that giving people the gift of time is not about letting them follow their bliss. "Every one of these things," he told the *New York Times*, "is just good business."[18] Perhaps that's why Patagonia gets nine hundred applications for every job opening.

Myth #3: Management's job is to assign and monitor the work.
Because Johnson was heading a volunteer group, she lacked the authority
to assign tasks. She could only invite people to sign on. But this in itself
is not a bad thing; people tend to give far more of themselves when
the work is offered rather than ordered. Just consider that in early
2009, SourceForge.net, a Web site where developers build open-source
software on their own time (and dime), listed 230,000 projects with more
than two million contributors.[19] The sole requirement for summoning
this vast army: allowing coders to *voluntarily* team up with other highly
motivated peers.

Although Johnson lacked a Web platform for open-sourcing talent,
she did leverage a powerful "technology": the gift of her idea. She
gave people the chance to pitch in on an exciting new opportunity,
in return for their talent, experience, and time. Her offer was by no
means limited to her immediate team. She extended the invitation
to Seventh Generation's sales brokers—in all, more than a hundred
additional people—and flew the volunteers to Chicago for a one-day
brainstorming session. Their goal: design the training modules for store
employees. Because the decision to attend was entirely theirs, the brokers
walked into the meeting with a high degree of enthusiasm—and zeal is
the catalyst for creativity.

Here, too, Johnson upended another management dictum: that
creativity comes only from "creative types"—people in R&D and marketing, not sales. In fact, Harvard professor Teresa Amabile's research
shows that innovative ideas can spring from any part of the organization. Creativity, she reports (as related in the previously cited *Fast
Company* article), depends on experience—which the brokers had in
abundance—as well as talent, the capacity "to think in new ways," and
especially "intrinsic motivation." Those who are "turned on by their
work," she argues, are far more likely to work creatively. The anecdotal
evidence from the brokers' brainstorming session suggests that Amabile
is on to something.

In an eight-hour span, the brokers, sales directors, and the Influencers
team threw their energy into the challenge; they crafted the design
principles for a program that would introduce store personnel to the

"Seven Truths of Seventh Generation." Having tapped the collective wisdom of the sales professionals, who spend as much time as anyone on grocery store floors, the team needed just a few short weeks to develop a prototype of a twenty-minute training module that included a short video and a facilitation guide.

The rationale for creating the prototype wasn't to fashion a close approximation of the finished product; the goal was to spark the kind of feedback that would help the team evaluate the program and make midflight corrections. In a sense, they built the prototype so they could think through the problem. Because the overall project was small and under-resourced, the team avoided the excessive gilding that so often drains a budget without adding much more in value.

The demo was still rough around the edges when it was tested in six cities, but that didn't matter; it quickly proved a hit. Surveys with the grocery teams and merchandisers showed that 85 percent thought the modules gave them "useful information" that would help them do their jobs better; more than 71 percent said they'd share the information with store customers "often."

The feedback also yielded two negative but invaluable insights. First, the name had to go. "Influencing the Influencer" sounded like brainwashing. After much work, the team came up with a new title: "GIVE—Generate Inspiration Via Education." And second, the video couldn't be a commercial for Seventh Generation. So the team broadened the thematic sweep to include issues like how to read the labels on cleaning products and how to care for newborns, and it recruited a highly credentialed pediatrician to narrate the videos.

In early 2007, when Johnson reported the results of her testing to the company's senior management, Seventh Generation's "proximate environment"—the changes in society and the economy that affect our business—had moved fortuitously in her favor. Al Gore's riveting documentary, *An Inconvenient Truth,* had just come out, and global climate change and sustainability were front and center on many people's personal radars. Shoppers were more than ready to turn into those center aisles and search out nontoxic alternatives to conventional packaged products. Thanks to GIVE, a small army of educated experts was ready to help them make knowledgeable, conscientious purchasing decisions. In GIVE's first year alone, it connected with more than 140,000 people.

"Now [GIVE] is moving from retail directly to the consumer," says Johnson. "Moms' groups are accessing these materials and passing them on to their friends. The whole thing is going viral."

Some Lessons

In the end, it was a no-brainer to hire two new sales directors and let Johnson step into her new job—as Seventh Generation's first-ever Director of Education. Already, she's laying plans to become our first Chief Knowledge Officer, a position in which she would ensure that the company's institutional knowledge, accumulated over more than two decades, is captured and available for Seventh Generation's next generation. Whether that comes to pass or not, Johnson's learning adventure has helped make our work culture less conventional, more purposeful, and certainly more responsible. And it delivers, for those who are willing to try, a few more lessons in community building:

- *Start small.* Like any smart researcher, Johnson tested her hypothesis with a simple experiment—her meeting with Whole Foods team leaders. When the results proved positive, she upped the ante—but only slightly—by requesting a modest budget to prototype the program. Had she somehow won a big budget for a high-profile launch (not likely), the project would have soaked up an inordinate amount of resources and executive attention. With all the excess baggage, it could easily have crashed.

- *Run the new effort along with the "now effort."* The company minimized the risk of putting a damper on sales by insisting that Johnson continue to head up our western sales operations, even as she took on this new project.

- *Recruit volunteers.* When people choose to do the work, they contribute their passion as well as their diligence. By inviting the brokers to participate, Johnson got more brains into the mix, which yielded better ideas.

- *Prototype.* When the team prototyped the "Influencers" program, they weren't just eliciting feedback, they were viscerally describing their strategy. Because the project was still in beta, the team minimized the number of permissions it needed from upper management, while it maximized the opportunities to learn—from staffers as well as stakeholders.

- *Stay aligned.* Seventh Generation is attempting to exert a gravitational pull on companies in our orbit—and beyond—to help them move in a sustainable direction. The GIVE program seeks to do the same with consumers. "We were totally in line with the purpose and the mission of the company," says Johnson. "More than anything, that's why we succeeded."

Susan Johnson's journey demonstrates that it is indeed possible for one person to help a responsible company bring out the best from its community. It reminds us that responsible revolutionaries strive to be as innovative with their people as they are with their R&D. Her lead has pushed Seventh Generation to experiment with letting other associates redefine their work—so long as they can make the business case for doing so. And we are testing to see how people can effectively devote some "120-percent time"—or perhaps even 20-percent time—to noncore projects. Equally powerfully, Johnson's odyssey is proof for all of us that there are indeed exits from career cul-de-sacs. All we need is the foresight and fortitude to grab the wheel and head for the road less traveled.

MAKE IT TRANSPARENT

IN A SEE-THROUGH WORLD, IT DOESN'T PAY TO BE OPAQUE

Try to imagine Coca-Cola revealing to the world its annual contribution to childhood obesity and tooth decay—and engaging its customers and stakeholders in a no-holds-barred discussion on how to take on the problem.

Attempt to conjure up, if you can, British Petroleum raising the curtain on the dark side of its refineries' safety performance, including the Texas plant where eighteen workers died in a recent three-year period.

Ponder Toyota convening an international conference to disclose its contribution to climate change and worldwide increases in smog-related asthma, allergies, and lung cancer.

Can't quite conceive it? How about this: picture Timberland, the outdoor footwear and clothing retailer, exposing the environmental imprint—including climate impact and chemical use—of many of its shoes.

That last scenario is not the stuff of pipe dreams. It's a real-world example of a company doing what's unnatural: publicly baring, for everyone to see, its good, bad, and ugly impacts on people and the planet. (Later in this chapter, we'll take a deeper look at the outfitter.) Like Timberland, a growing number of companies are adopting a new model of corporate behavior: to be a good global citizen, you've got to live in a glass house.[1]

TRANSPARENCY'S ASCENDANCY

Thanks to the democratizing effect of the Web in general and blogs in particular—as well as outside pressure from activist groups, nongovernmental organizations (NGOs), the media, and citizen stakeholders—the traditional corporate communications model has been flipped. A company's communications no longer flows exclusively from the top down, with only executives in the C-suite permitted to make "official" pronouncements via press release. The public airing of company business also flows from the bottom up—and out—as front-line associates tweet and blog not only on the routine minutiae of day-to-day life in the cubes, but also about management practices, product development, strategy, and everything else that the company is up to—wrong as well as right.

If anything, transparency has hit the top of the org chart. Big-dog executives ranging from Sun Microsystems' Jonathan Schwartz to HDNet's Mark Cuban to Jet Blue's former chief, David Neeleman, have seized on the Web to vent, dish, deliberate, debate, and issue mea culpas. (It's axiomatic that in this age of MySpace and YouTube confessionals, conceding your mistakes makes you stronger.) A few examples:

- Google has long encouraged its engineers to blog liberally about their projects—no surprise there—but so too has Microsoft, "once a paragon of buttoned-down control," as *Wired* described it.[2]
- No company has used Twitter to advance transparency quite like the Internet apparel retailer Zappos, whose employees are power users and whose CEO, Tony Hsieh, has drawn more than a million followers.

- The insurance giant Aflac has decided that it no longer pays to cover up the controversial issue of CEO compensation; instead, it petitions shareholders to approve by vote the newly public salaries of its senior executives.

- InnoCentive, a spin-off from Eli Lilly, taps an online network of more than seventy thousand scientists around the world to crack technical challenges that have stumped internal R&D teams. The logic of inviting a global mob of brainiacs to pick through your "secrets" is inescapable: more contributors increase the likelihood that you'll net sharper insights, information, and ideas than you could ever glean on your own.

There's no denying that exposing secrets and revealing blemishes runs against the grain of conventional business wisdom. Transparency is scary; it's not what most businesspeople are prepared for. Such practices might seem both radical and impractical, but they are rapidly moving into the mainstream.

Transparency is becoming a core requirement for any company that aspires to do more than increase shareholder wealth. No less a blue-chip outfit than Big Blue itself has sung the praises of transparency. A February 2008 report from IBM Global Services argues that the extent to which a company is willing to open itself up to "stakeholder scrutiny" will be a "make or break factor in achieving CSR objectives."[3] The report underlines the notion that the powerful disinfectant that is transparency reduces a company's challenges by exposing them to the harsh light of day: "The company that invites more eyes on its operations can preempt problems that would otherwise become very expensive to solve."

TO ENSURE TRUST, BUILD TRANSPARENCY

When an organization aspires to create value by competing on values, it's doubly important to let the sun shine not only on its accomplishments but also on its less-than-flattering secrets and even its failures. Stakeholders expect responsible companies to be responsive—that is, open, candid, and engaged. After all, we work and compete in a reputation economy; for a company that holds itself out as a model of responsible behavior, reputation means everything.

A 2003 survey of C-level execs at the World Economic Forum's 34th annual meeting in Davos, Switzerland, found that "reputation" was the second-most important measure of a corporation's success—only "quality of products or services" scored higher. In a December 2008 McKinsey survey of CFOs, investment professionals, and finance professionals, more than 75 percent agreed that "maintaining a good corporate reputation or brand equity is the most important way that [CR] programs create value."[4] The art of cost-effectively managing invaluable intangible assets like reputation and respect starts with transparency.

Common sense suggests, and data affirms, that the more consumers perceive a company as trustworthy, the more goods and services it will sell. In 2009, when Ponzi schemes and bank bailouts plunged the public's regard for business to an all-time nadir, the Edelman Trust Barometer—an annual survey of "global opinion leaders"—found that 91 percent of adults said they bought a product or service from companies they regarded as reputable; 77 percent refused to buy from companies they regarded as louche. Reputation matters, both to the brand's value and to its top line.

Just as trust burnishes a brand's reputation, transparency builds trust. Trustworthy companies reveal what other companies often hide. Companies that consistently communicate the good—and, even more important, the bad—of their business operations and treatment of their workforce are more likely to be regarded as credible.[5] In noting a clear link between reputation, trust, and transparency, the 2009 Edelman survey concluded, "transparency . . . is as important to reputation as 'value for money' and [a] 'strong financial future.'"[6] If it's true that CEOs really do value reputational capital, they'd better get used to wearing plastic wrap.

TURNING CRITICS INTO COLLABORATORS

The whole point of being transparent is to not only reveal problems but also to solve them. By leveraging the transparency imperative, you tap into the crowd's ideas as well as its critiques—and create the opportunity to parlay adversarial relationships into fruitful partnerships. Anyone who doubts this need only recall the recent histories of Nike and Gap—how each company, by putting out warts-and-all reports on working conditions in its contract factories, eventually forged solutions-oriented compacts with some of its harshest critics.

If Home Depot, for example, had been transparent about its (former) use of old-growth lumber in its products, the big-box retailer might well have avoided a protracted assault from rain-forest conservation activists and instead moved more quickly toward the inevitable old-growth phase-out. If Monsanto had revealed its plans to launch genetically modified food products in Europe, stakeholders might have pushed it to self-correct in time to snuff the blowback from activists and consumers that followed. On second thought, perhaps even transparency couldn't have spared Monsanto from the wrath of European activists decrying "Frankenfoods." But you get the idea. If more companies understood what transpires when bloggers, consumers, and activists put a microscope to their carefully concealed operations, they would seize on the power of transparency to help them achieve their business goals—without taking such big hits to their reputations and their balance sheets.

No company that we are aware of lives entirely in that idealized glass house, accepting the transparency challenge at every level of the organization. Some secrets—Coke's formula, Apple's design process, Cisco's M&A strategy—will inevitably remain closeted. But as the accelerating power of viral media continues to upend every organization's ability to control its message, even companies that seek to act sustainably are finding that the pursuit of full-frontal transparency is often unnerving and sometimes painful—as we can attest.

THE COST OF IGNORING THE TRANSPARENCY IMPERATIVE

One morning in mid-March 2008, Seventh Generation's senior management team awoke to these hellacious headlines:

SEVENTH GENERATION BATTLES CARCINOGENIC CHEMICAL CONTROVERSY

"ORGANIC" AND "NATURAL" CONSUMER PRODUCTS FOUND CONTAMINATED WITH CANCER-CAUSING CHEMICAL

The Organic Consumers Association, a public interest nonprofit, had released a report showing that forty-seven organic and natural consumer products contained detectable levels of the contaminate 1,4-dioxane. Seventh Generation's dish liquid was one of the brands named in the study. This revelation challenged our honesty and threatened one of our most valuable assets: our reputation.

Of course, we would not intentionally add 1,4-dioxane to our dish liquid. As the *Los Angeles Times* noted, the compound is a byproduct of a process used to improve the degreasing agent in detergents. Our manufacturers vacuum strip the dioxane to minute levels; the OCA report showed that in terms of 1,4-dioxane, our dish liquid was the safest of all the dish liquids tested. That said, we didn't argue with the OCA's core assertion. We agreed that 1,4-dioxane doesn't belong in our products—the by-product is not consistent with who we are and what we stand for.

Having worked for more than five years to remove dioxane from our dish products as well as our laundry products, we were saddened to see our incomplete progress characterized as a dishonest act. But the truth is that our effort was simply not good enough. Not because we hadn't yet succeeded in getting rid of dioxane—working with our supplier, we've since eliminated the contaminant from our products. Our real mistake was to exclude consumers and key stakeholders from our ongoing dialogue about dioxane. The problem wasn't high-lighted on our Web site or detailed in our earlier corporate responsibility report. In short, we flunked the transparency test.

And therein lies the larger lesson about what it takes to be a transparent company. We had hundreds of meetings and conversations about how to purge dioxane. We ran many of our own tests and worked closely with suppliers and manufacturers. But we didn't take that one necessary step: to share our trials and tribulations with everyone outside the company who might have wanted to weigh in, express concerns, ask questions, and challenge our progress.

Five or six years ago, the expectations about transparency were somewhat more relaxed than they are today. Perhaps we hoped that by the time 1,4-dioxane became a public issue, we would have found a way to completely vanquish it (exactly the wrong approach). But dioxane endured, and in the rush to confront an unceasing array of new challenges and opportunities, we never took a hard look at whether to publicly discuss the problem. In a sense, our dioxane dilemma got "grandfathered in" under a new set of transparency rules. Predictably and painfully, it was soon revealed to the outside world. The breathless headlines quickly followed.

Many of us at Seventh Generation had spent our careers working to avoid just such an experience. But viewed another way, dioxane presented us with a rather extreme opportunity to absorb the new rules about transparency—and to seek out innovators that have dared to wear the see-through.

GREEN IS THE COLOR OF TRANSPARENCY: PATAGONIA

When a company begins to make itself transparent, it conducts an unblinking audit of not only its financials, but all its activities. The process is analogous to the lifecycle analysis of a product. Just as many product-development teams put a spotlight on all the impacts of a new offering to evaluate its sustainability, the company casts a bright light on itself by measuring the total, systemic effects of its behavior and operations on global climate change, human rights, energy, water, the local community, and anything else that might attract stakeholders' curiosity. The result is a 3-D picture of the organization's successes, but more important, of its flaws, its vulnerabilities—anything that poses a risk to its reputation.

Probably no company has spent more time calculating and mapping its greatest negative effects than Patagonia, the pioneering maker of outdoor apparel and gear.[7] Patagonia chalked up $315 million in sales for fiscal year 2009, a number that does not begin to limn the size of its influence. As *Fortune* has noted, "from day one, Patagonia has punched above its weight"[8] by making the big outdoors accessible to consumers and by advancing the idea that business can do far more good than we care to imagine. Patagonia has also been among the vanguard of the comparatively few companies that have dared to wear the see-through. The notion that companies should operate with "maximum transparency" is written into the "Our Values" statement that the deep ecologist Jerry Mander long ago penned for Patagonia. And maximum transparency was one of the catalysts that spurred the company to embark on its version of a life-cycle analysis, one of the earliest efforts by any U.S. company to take a hard, uncompromising look at the environmental toll of its activities.

For Patagonia, a core value is the Socratic imperative to "lead an examined life"—to ask tough questions, delve into deviously difficult problems, and push for solutions. After all, before you can act transparently you first must understand deeply what needs to be revealed. And so it was that in 1991 the Ventura, California–based company set about casting a cold eye on the environmental footprint of the four major fibers that go into its wares: wool, polyester, nylon, and cotton. As Patagonia founder Yvon Chouinard told us, they knew even before the study that the petroleum-based synthetics were obvious enviro-villains. The big surprise was that the creation of so-called "natural" products made from cotton and wool was every bit as bad.

Transparency Leads to Accountability

Chouinard dispatched a team of environmental-impact scouts to bird-dog the company's wool and cotton supply chains all the way back to their respective sources. The team soon learned that wool soaks up chemicals at each stage of its processing, from the pesticide-laced sheep dips to the chlorine bleaching of the yarn to the use of heavy metal-based dyes. Conventionally grown cotton is even worse: it annually consumes 25 percent of the world's insecticides and 10 percent of its pesticides—many of whose chemical components were originally formulated as nerve gases for warfare. For an outfit whose fundamental raison d'être is to "inspire and implement solutions to the environmental crisis,"[9] chemically grown cotton was a poison pill that could potentially weaken the brand and afflict the company's core principles.

Patagonia could have wormed its way around the cotton conundrum, as had virtually every other apparel maker at the time. Instead, it followed its injunction to think through the problem, find a just principle, and apply it. "The stuff is evil," said Chouinard, when we met with him in a conference room at the company's headquarters. "The more we studied it, the more we were determined to never use traditionally grown cotton fiber again."[10] Thanks to the founder's prodding, Patagonia's board of directors voted to dump conventional cotton and switch to 100-percent organic. But a quick analysis showed that the world supply of organically grown cotton was too small to meet the company's needs. To adopt "good cotton," Patagonia would have to convert farmers and clothing manufacturers to the good-cotton cause. Rather than deflect scrutiny of its contribution to environmental degradation, Patagonia *invited* it. Only then could it hope to persuade others to help crack the problem. So Patagonia . . .

. . . *open-sourced the dark side of its performance.* The company distributed the results of its environmental impact study, including a chart listing the toxic effects of the major cotton pesticides used in the United States, to anyone who asked for it—customers, consumers, and competitors.

. . . *made it real.* The organic-agriculture activist Will Allen led a busload of Patagonia's apparel-manufacturing reps on a tour of cotton farms in the San Joaquin Valley, where they walked the chemically sterilized earth and, at one memorable stop, nearly got sprayed by a crop duster.

. . . *made it personal.* Chouinard contributed a stirring essay to the Spring 1996 edition of Patagonia's catalog and later authored a classic business memoir, *Let My People Go Surfing,* in which he mapped out the moral case for going organic. "Not to do so," he wrote, "would have been unconscionable."[11]

. . . *took responsibility.* That same year, the company held a three-day conference for everyone who contributed to the creation and sale of Patagonia products. An introductory video underlined Patagonia's flinty resolve to assume responsibility for its own actions: "It is not

OK to assign blame for environmental degradation elsewhere—the production, distribution, and use of Patagonia products is causing damage."[12]

Face Facts: "Green" Companies Pollute

In the spring of 1996, when cotton sportswear amounted to 20 percent of its business, Patagonia stepped into the unknown. After spending two hard years reinventing its supply chain, it switched to all-organic cotton. Because clothing made from organic cotton required a premium price, the move sparked a 20-percent decline in sales. But eventually the company right-sized itself by demonstrating to consumers that it's better to pay a little more up front for organic cotton than to postpone even higher payments for the hidden environmental costs of chemical cotton. Along the way, Patagonia built a better-quality line of clothing, stayed aligned with its principles, and influenced far bigger companies, such as Levi Strauss and Wal-Mart, to follow its lead.

Perhaps the most enduring outcome from Patagonia's cotton odyssey is that the effort to transparently and truthfully plumb the environmental consequences of its actions pushed it to declare, as Chouinard memorably asserted in his book, that "everything we make pollutes. But we were all surprised at how bad the news was; *sustainable manufacturing* is an oxymoron."[13] In a sense, the environmental impact assessment led Patagonia to publicly acknowledge what it privately intuited: If you are in the business of making things, as Chouinard once put it in an interview with *TreeHugger*, "no matter how clean and green [you] try to be, [you] are still a net polluter."[14] Don't try to kid yourself into thinking that you aren't.

Tell Your Story

Patagonia's most ambitious experiment with radical transparency grew out of its frustration with conventional corporate responsibility reporting—a voluntary effort by companies to hold themselves accountable to a higher ethical standard. In 2004, Patagonia produced a CR audit based on the Global Reporting Initiative, which was developed for large, primarily public companies. The GRI seeks to document, at a granular level, a company's social and environmental footprint. Many regard it as the gold standard in CR reporting. Iconoclastic Patagonia had a different take.

The effort to gather all of the GRI's compliance data and assemble it into a standardized format proved an enormous time sink. And when the work was completed, no one liked the result. The published document felt antiseptic and inauthentic. Chouinard pronounced it "absolute bullshit." Jill Dumain, Patagonia's director of environmental analysis, gave it just a slightly more diplomatic review. "It was as boring as all the other reports out there—it felt like a marketing statement," she recalls. "We weren't challenged to put in the tough stuff—the areas where we failed. We printed out twelve copies for our board, and after that, our corporate social responsibility reporting died an appropriate death."

What survived was the desire to share—in a way that felt true to Patagonia's tell-it-like-it-is culture—an unflinching account of the environmental and social effects of every link in its supply chain. That instinct gained a real sense of urgency when Dumain sat in on a workshop led by Tim Kitchin, then a director of AccountAbility, a London-based sustainable-development consultancy.

As the Supply of Information Increases, So Too Does the Demand

Kitchin presented survey data showing that UK consumers, by wielding the Web as a powerful research tool, were rapidly becoming far savvier about dissecting and evaluating a brand's social and environmental performance. Having armed themselves with more knowledge, consumers were no longer relying solely on watchdog groups, such as professional activists and NGOs, to hold companies accountable. They were taking their questions and concerns straight to the source—the companies themselves. Those companies that were more forthcoming—that is, more transparent—were viewed as more credible.

Kitchin's research resonated powerfully with Dumain's own experience. Consumers' questions about the provenance of Patagonia's products were rapidly becoming more sophisticated. Any customer-service rep could knock back a softball question like "Why are you doing business in China?" But increasingly, Patagonia was whiffing on the fastballs: "What are you doing about your China-based manufacturers, who use electricity from coal-fired energy plants that spew tons of heat-trapping gases across Asia?" For that, Patagonia just didn't have a good answer.

Dumain's anecdotal evidence, combined with Kitchin's data, seemed to suggest an axiom: as the Internet supplies consumers with unprecedented amounts of product and company information, the demand for even better information increases. Better insights spur smarter conversations, which yield new questions and a desire for more communication. Given that the Web was fueling consumers' desire to learn more, Patagonia decided that it would use its Web site to tell more.

A Truly Transparent Company Is Its Own Harshest Critic

In the spring of 2007, Dumain teamed up with Rick Ridgeway, Patagonia's head honcho for environmental initiatives, and a small band of Web heads to create an interactive microsite at patagonia.com. The site, which launched in the fall of that year, is called "The Footprint Chronicles." It is among the boldest bids by any company for greater transparency. Chronicles refutes the notion that conventional corporate responsibility reporting represents the limits of responsible—that is, open and accountable—corporate behavior. For that reason alone, the thinking behind the Footprint Chronicles is worth a deeper look.

"It all started with a different question," recalls Ridgeway. "Instead of writing a report, what if we created a Web site that let people go through our supply chain and see video and photos of the people who make our products? But most importantly, they hear about where we're doing better and where we're failing. Maybe they'd help us improve."

To build the site, the Chronicles team drew on scouting reports from a crew of Patagonia sleuths who traveled the world. The group traced the evolution of five products, as they made their way from the designers' sketchpads in Ventura to New Zealand's sheep ranches to Patagonia's Asia-based factories to delivery in its Reno, Nevada, distribution center. The team studied weavers in Bangkok, interviewed the manager of a fifty-thousand-employee shoe factory in Dongguan, China, and toured a fiber-making plant in North Carolina. Their video and field notes helped the Web team create an interactive map of the world, which offers an uncompromising look at the environmental toll of manufacturing and transporting Patagonia's wares. Click on the Wool 2 Crew, for example, and you trace the shirt's travels across more than sixteen thousand miles, from New Zealand to Japan to California and finally, Nevada. Patagonia's terse verdict on its shirt's globe-spanning journey: "This is not sustainable."

The site cuts through the great swaths of data that so often over-whelm conventional CR reporting by homing in on the environmental impacts that matter most: miles traveled, waste produced, carbon dioxide emitted, and energy consumed. And it gives the data some clear-eyed context. When it's reported that Patagonia's production of a single down sweater burns up 9.4 kWh of energy, you also learn that that amount is equal to burning an eighteen-watt compact fluorescent lightbulb for twenty-two days straight.

Whereas companies too often slink past the bad news in their cor-porate responsibility reporting, Chronicles confronts it head on, through two boxes appropriately titled "The Good" and "The Bad." The Good, for example, billboards the Puckerware Shirt's "air-conditioned drape" and "easy care"; The Bad gives equal, spin-free space to the shirt's total lack of recycled content in its polyester, which failed its initial lab test. And a box titled "What We Think" doesn't try to paint a sunny eco-future for the shirt. "We don't yet know for sure," concedes Patagonia, "when we can switch to recycled [poly] fabric."

Chronicles is still very much a work in progress. Its snapshots of Patagonia's logistics and manufacturing operations strike some com-mentators as too superficial.[15] And Patagonia sometimes glosses over the blemishes, as when it reveals neither the name nor the toxicity of the synthetic finish that "persists in the environment" but nevertheless con-tinues to coat its Nine Trails Shorts. Yet those flaws somehow make the site a little more authentic—or at least, a little more human. "The essential thing was to have the bad as well as the good," says Chouinard. "Otherwise, it just would have been greenwashing."

From Confrontations to Productive Conversations

Trading in a three-piece suit for the see-through hasn't quite hit the mainstream of business fashion. For the majority of companies, radical transparency is still too discomforting to try on. Even bold, brash Patagonia, which is sometimes aggressively anticorporate—Ridgeway has publicly described conventional businesspeople as "greaseballs," and Chouinard has declared that he's "never respected the profession"—at first found it difficult to accept full-on transparency.

Although Ridgeway and Chouinard were strong proponents of bringing a high degree of transparency to the Footprint Chronicles, some associates were allergic to the idea. An especially inflammatory issue was how to handle perfluorooctanoic acid, or PFOA, a chemical compound that accumulates in the bloodstream and at higher exposures may be carcinogenic. PFOA shows up in the water-repellent finish on Patagonia's outerwear; its revelation would no doubt alarm some of the company's deep-green consumers. Patagonia's customer-service reps fretted that spotlighting PFOA would spark a surge of phone calls from uneasy shoppers. The R&D folks argued that they should at least be able to post, on the Chronicles' site, their plan for ridding products of PFOA. "For a lot of people," acknowledges Dumain, "transparency was very scary."

In the end, staffers had reason to worry—but not as much as they'd feared. In the fall of 2007, when the Footprint Chronicles went live, it indeed drew some disparaging email. After learning through the Web site that the Eco Rain Shell jacket was coated with PFOA, a rash of irate consumers fired off notes insisting that "Eco" be struck from the product's label. Yet the pushback proved helpful. It put an exclamation point on the notion that consumers were seriously concerned about PFOA, and that Patagonia had better redouble its efforts to eliminate it.

For the most part, the negative news prompted positive comments; the majority of posters to the Chronicles' blog praised Patagonia for its aggressive honesty. By issuing a reasonably frank accounting of its progress and its setbacks, Patagonia found that many of its customers were more forgiving than it had anticipated. "Transparency defuses conflict," says Dumain. "Issues like PFOA, which might have led to confrontations, have instead prompted fruitful conversations."

But why? It's not unreasonable to expect that by identifying a suspected carcinogen such as PFOA, Patagonia was inviting a crush of criticism. Why did the exact opposite prove (mostly) true?

Partly, it's because transparency helps companies behave proactively rather than reactively. When a company is the lead investigator of its own performance, it gives itself a better shot at getting ahead of societal concerns. Such was the case in the mid-1990s, when Patagonia alerted its industry to the heinous effects of industrial cotton and led the move to organics.

But there's also the human side of the transparency story. We value honesty and accountability; we abhor mendacity and resist secrecy. We appreciate those companies that attempt to investigate their imperfections, identify the culprits—the conventional cotton and the PFOAs of the world—and take a real stab at cracking the case. The essayist Alex Steffen gets this when he writes, "The shape of a sustainable company is still a mystery. What folks in the corporate world need to remember is that in any mystery, we all want to root for the detectives."[16]

With an opaque company, the heroes are the outside investigators—the activists who sniff out the company's misdeeds. With a transparent company there is, at least potentially, just one hero—the company itself.

THE USER'S GUIDE TO TRANSPARENCY: TIMBERLAND AND NOVO NORDISK

"In early 2006, [we] made the difficult decision to leave a Chinese factory that accounted for 17% of our production. It was a bitter pill to swallow—especially since our business relationship had lasted ten years. The jobs of hundreds of workers in China were put at risk when [we] ceased production . . . And because we weren't able to 'Make it better' for them . . . we failed."[17]

MAKING PATAGONIA'S FOOTPRINT CHRONICLES

Three design principles were followed in building Patagonia's transparency machine, the Footprint Chronicles:

Success breeds that powerful motivator called fear. The effort to launch the Footprint Chronicles got a jolt of adrenaline when the April 2007 issue of *Fortune* featured Chouinard on its cover and pronounced Patagonia "the coolest company on the planet." It was a PR bonanza, and that was a problem. Although pleased with the recognition, staffers were queasy over the possibility that the celebrity treatment could prove to be a contrarian indicator. "We felt like people were writing a glowing CR report for us," says Dumain. "There was a concern that if we didn't tell the other side of the story, the stuff we were struggling with, we could really be set up for a backlash." In a sense, Patagonia's fear of the article's repercussions overcame its fear of transparency.

Perfection is not required. Despite the surfer ambience of its workplace, Patagonia is filled with unapologetic perfectionists — an ideal quality for making high-risk sports gear, but not so desirable for launching a warts-and-all transparency initiative. Mindful of Patagonia's tendency toward analysis paralysis, Chouinard and Ridgeway counseled the Chronicles team to "learn out loud in public." Their message: break from Patagonia's tendency to have an answer for every question, and get used to posing questions for which there are no easy answers. Only then could they begin to enlist consumers' help in crafting solutions.

Write tight. The Footprint Chronicles is ultra-stingy on its word count. The boxes listing the environmental pros and cons of Patagonia's apparel allow for just a couple of lines of copy — a Twitter tweet, by comparison, seems downright novelistic. And that is by design. There's no space for explanations and justifications. Context is clutter; excuses are excluded. What remains are simply the unadorned, unvarnished facts of each product's environmental impact.

These blunt, unsparing words accurately capture the brio of the privately held, renegade outfit that launched the Footprint Chronicles. Except they didn't come from Patagonia. The quotation's source is the 2006 Corporate Social Responsibility report issued by the Timberland Company.

With roughly six thousand employees working across the United States, Europe, and Asia, and 2008 revenues of $1.36 billion, Timberland is far larger than Patagonia and certainly more mainstream. In a speech, Rick Ridgeway once declared that Patagonia's shareholders are "the wild places and the wild animals."[18] Timberland's shareholders, on the other hand, are the human owners of Timberland stock, which is traded on the NYSE. Understandably, those shareholders might well look askance at any unquiet declarations of "failure." Yet in its pursuit of radical transparency, Timberland is almost as fearless and arguably as innovative as Patagonia.

Timberland hasn't kicked over the conventional approach to operating transparently so much as it's kicked that process into overdrive. The company has moved from issuing unhurried annual CSR reports to fast-forward, quarterly updates of key performance indicators. It has cut through the complexity of those lengthy reports by developing a "Green Index" tag, modeled on a nutrition label, which gives consumers a quick take on how some products rate in terms of their impact on the environment. (More on this later in the chapter.) And it has moved from "corporate statement" to "stakeholder engagement"[19] by launching quarterly phone dialogues with CEO Jeffrey Swartz, in which callers can zero in on critical issues of the moment, such as eco-labeling and sustainable sourcing.

"Transparency is about urgency," Swartz told us when we met him at the company's Stratham, New Hampshire, headquarters. "It's a recognition that the world is in an environmental crisis, our company is part of the problem, and we're going to lose our permission to have a relationship with consumers if we don't fix things *now*."[20]

Novo Nordisk A/S, a Danish health-care company that supplies the majority of the world's insulin, is another big, fast-moving pioneer in innovating corporate transparency. True, it's more circumspect than its boisterous American counterparts, Timberland and Patagonia. The anecdotal evidence suggests that the larger the company, the less likely that it will flag its social and environmental shortcomings, and this rough maxim applies to Novo. Given its 2008 revenues of $7.96 billion and a market cap in the neighborhood of $29 billion, you're unlikely to find any eye-opening admissions of failure in the drug maker's corporate responsibility communications.

But not many companies are better exemplars of this notion: transparency doesn't co-opt skeptics, but it does preempt them. Novo Nordisk understands that activists have less to criticize when a company is already announcing its mistakes. By acting with clarity and candor, a company can start the process of enlisting critics in the bid to improve its social and environmental record—people who are already attempting to x-ray the firm, whether it likes it or not.

For Novo Nordisk, more prying eyes ultimately mean fewer festering problems. Novo may well be the only pharmaceutical to feature a section on bioethics on its Web site. This gives activists and NGOs a sizable peephole into the company's practices in such controversial areas as animal experimentation, stem-cell research, and gene technology—the first step toward turning critics into collaborators. Novo also uses a team of crack trend-spotters to track the entire agenda of social issues and alert senior management as to when it needs to wrap a bit more of the see-through around a prickly problem. And it brings its critics in by meeting regularly with animal-welfare activists and other groups.

"Stakeholders are constantly challenging our bioethical work," says Lise Holst, Novo's director of bioethics. "And we are happy that they do so. You can't have a fruitful dialogue without transparency. And transparency is worthless if it doesn't lead to dialogue."

By now, you're probably wondering whether your company is immodest enough or counterintuitive enough to see the advantages in going naked, like a Novo Nordisk, a Timberland, or even a Patagonia. But assuming it is, how might that happen? How can you build a transparency imperative into your organization when you're not the CEO and not everyone dares to climb out of the foxhole and welcome outside critics when they start gunning?

Anyone who contemplates building a crystalline culture quickly bumps up against a jarring set of questions: How do I make the business case? How do I defuse detractors and win advocates? What are the risks—and the game plan? And what about the fear factor?

Fact is, those questions are never entirely resolved. Achieving real transparency is a revolutionary goal, but it's an iterative journey. We can't predict whether any company will ever be *sufficiently* transparent. It may well be an unattainable ideal, because society's expectations of corporate transparency are constantly changing. The moment you think you have arrived, you have failed. Transparency is not a state of being; it's an endless process of becoming.

Neither out-there outfits like Patagonia nor more mainstream innovators like Timberland and Novo Nordisk are perfect, invincible heralds of a new transparency order. But they are confronting transparency's most intractable challenges, and they are making real progress. They demonstrate that it's possible to publicly acknowledge setbacks, collaborate with critics, and still run a successful global business. And they offer a host of hard-won lessons, both salutary and cautionary, for building a business culture that's more see-through than see-nothing.

Seize the Crisis

These words have been attributed to Stanford economist Paul Romer: "[A] crisis is a terrible thing to waste."[21] The line has been so often cited during our recent crisis-buffeted times, it's become a well-worn cliché. Yet like many a hoary adage, sometimes there's real truth in it. In the case of Timberland and Novo Nordisk, both companies reacted to strikingly similar near-calamities by using them to push toward greater transparency.

In the 1990s, Timberland watched with growing alarm as protesters denounced two of the giants in its industry—Nike and Gap—for sweatshop conditions in their suppliers' factories. At first, both big brands reacted defensively (though that would certainly change), which only invited more probing from activists. As additional problems were uncovered, Nike and Gap became prominent symbols of corporate negligence and greed. Timberland wasn't targeted in the same aggressive way, but activists could easily have decided that it also deserved their wrath.

"We use similar sourcing processes as other brands, which made us just as vulnerable," says Beth Holzman, Timberland's manager of CSR strategy and reporting. "That realization really started a lot of conversations about what we could publicly divulge."

The 1990s proved to be an even tougher time for Novo Nordisk. Animal-welfare activists shot undercover video of animals housed in deplorable conditions in the company's contract laboratories, and they released the footage to the Danish media. That sparked a near-nationwide outcry and a protest at the company's headquarters in a suburb outside Copenhagen.

Novo's reaction was a singular example of business as unusual. Company representatives met with their adversaries to hear their complaints firsthand. Not long after, Novo Nordisk organized the first of many sit-downs with activists, including the Danish Animal Welfare Society and other groups, which led to a long-standing collaboration and world-leading standards for humanely housing experimental animals.

Increasingly, companies are finding themselves enmeshed in larger ecosystems, whereby the actions of one entity—such as a contract factory or an independent lab—reflect on the larger whole. The super-sized brands in the U.S. apparel industry, Nike and Gap, learned this firsthand, when the sweatshop issue became an international scandal that (for a time) scorched their reputations and their performance. For Timberland and Novo Nordisk, their respective crises became opportunities to fully reckon with the notion that a company can't be responsible, and it certainly can't be transparent, if its community—its suppliers, manufacturers, and even its competitors—remains opaque. When bad news befell their companies, they didn't waste it.

Make the Case

Early on, there was a sizable group inside Novo Nordisk that wouldn't warm to the idea of convening with a bunch of hot-headed animal-welfare zealots. The skeptics, many of whom were front-line scientists, argued that the activists would only criticize and make unrealistic requests. In their view, a meeting wouldn't lead to anything constructive; it would simply stir up a lot of trouble. It took a lot of back-and-forth before the naysayers' real worries were revealed: if Novo caved to the activists' demands, the company's research might well be impeded.

That, of course, was a nontrivial concern. We are living in a time when the rate of change is surging and competitive advantage is ebbing; no drug maker can afford any kind of drag on its R&D initiatives. But in Novo Nordisk's view, that was a risk it had to take. After further internal discussions, a rough consensus began to emerge: although meeting with the activists might threaten Novo's research, not meeting with them might threaten Novo's reputation.

"We are a research-based company, and drug development presently includes animal experimentation and testing," says Holst. "It's also a legal requirement. But if society doesn't allow us to do what we need to do, we are finished. To win society's approval, we must engage with stakeholders on controversial issues such as animal testing. And we must be transparent about it."*

Win Allies

The debate within Novo Nordisk over whether to start a dialogue with animal welfare groups wasn't confined to a corporate crèche or an isolated CR team. The conversation extended to the highest levels of the organization. The people who were in favor of dialogue were more

---

*Seventh Generation strongly opposes any and all uses of animal testing and supports all efforts to develop alternatives to animal testing and experimentation. This is a fundamental part of our mission and values. Novo Nordisk is arguably the most progressive of any large drug maker in regard to testing on animals, but we respectfully disagree with its position. To learn more about Seventh Generation's policy on animal experimentation, visit the "Ask a Question" feature at our Web site, http://www.seventhgeneration.com/. To learn more about the Novo Nordisk position on animal research, see its publication, "Animals in Pharmaceutical Research and Development," http://www.novonordisk.com/images/science/Bioethics/Downloads/Bioethics_Animals%20UK_25-09.pdf.

convincing, not least because they had more power. That fact ensured that the final decision came with senior management's imprimatur and therefore carried real weight. With buy-in from the company's top leaders, the mid-tier skeptics had the cover they needed to opt in.

Let's face it. As long as senior managers are unwilling to do some arm-twisting, it's exceedingly difficult to win allies for the not-so-mainstream notion that a company should build a glass house and put out the welcome mat for its adversaries. The surest way to secure executive-level commitment to a transparency initiative is to demonstrate that it's an issue that's of grave concern to at least one group of key stakeholders. Regardless of whether the problem involves animal testing, climate change, or children slaving on a factory line in China, if it directly threatens a company's reputation and its bottom line, senior management will act fast.

Novo Nordisk employs a powerful tool called the "Learning Curve" to track the evolution of a societal issue that might threaten the company. The early stages are when it's most critical to take action, though as the sustainability expert Simon Zadek notes in a *Harvard Business Review* article, it's then that issues are still vague "and their potential significance well below conventional thresholds [that are] used . . . to determine materiality."[22]

Though the wider business community is often dismissive of issues in these first latent stages, this is exactly the moment when a company should connect with social activists—or as Zadek calls them, "nontraditional sources of knowledge." Activists and NGOs amplify the "faint signals" of oncoming change. By interacting with agenda-setting groups on the culture's frontier, you can get a clearer read on your industry's future. If you wait until an issue matures and a first mover seizes on it, it's too late. Observes Zadek: "Once leading companies adopt unconventional commitments . . . around certain societal issues [such as a set of labor standards for suppliers or the goal of going carbon-neutral], laggards must either follow suit or risk the consequences."

So the next time you propose a meeting with those supposedly unruly, underinformed activists, and you get some pushback from skeptical colleagues, let them decide: do they want the company to lead or to lag?

TRANSPARENCY STRESS TEST: MEETING WITH ADVERSARIES

How can you convince your skeptical colleagues that it's better to openly engage with outside critics than to shut them out? Lise Holst, bioethics chief for the Danish pharmaceutical Novo Nordisk, makes the case.

- *Reality check.* "If you can't face the world and openly talk about your company's activities," says Holst, "you're doing something wrong."
- *Debate, and educate.* "Sometimes, your critics aren't particularly well-informed, particularly in regard to scientific research. When you engage with people, you have an opportunity to correct their misperceptions."
- *From antipathy to empathy.* "When there's no personal connection, it's very easy to dislike people. A dialogue gives each person a chance to develop real empathy for the other's point of view."
- *Douse the spark before it flames.* "You see it in the United Kingdom — animal-rights activists and pharmaceutical companies are very aggressive towards each other. If you let an issue become highly polarized, it's almost impossible to reach agreement."

Collaborate with Critics

There's another reason why Novo Nordisk decided to open up and meet with animal-welfare groups: it knew that in the main, they were right. After launching its own investigation, the company found that the housing conditions for animals in its contract labs were, in fact, woefully inadequate. So the company's inaugural meeting with the Danish Animal Welfare Society, along with experts from the UK-based Royal Society for the Prevention of Cruelty to Animals and the Universities Federation for Animal Welfare, had a real purpose, and it wasn't to score debate points. It was to explore ways to forge a partnership, so as to develop improved standards for housing animals and a set of principles for their use in experiments and testing. "The goal was to seriously discuss the issue," recalls Holst, "and move in the direction that society wanted us to move in."

Novo Nordisk's interaction with these groups has not been frictionless; there've been plenty of moments when the two sides disagreed, disagreeably. But for the most part their one-of-a-kind partnership has proved fruitful. It produced a set of standards for housing animals that was later incorporated into the Council of Europe's revised guidelines on the protection of animals used in research.[23] It created both an audit process on the use of animals at contract labs and an internal committee to review all of Novo's animal studies—an industry first. And it led to what was most likely another first: a joint presentation between a drug-maker and an animal-welfare group at a pharmaceutical industry conference.

The evolution of Novo Nordisk's partnership with its former adversaries provides useful lessons for anyone who wants to use transparency to transform stakeholders into advocates and critics into allies. Novo is making real progress because the company . . .

. . . *didn't treat its first meeting with animal-welfare groups as its only meeting.* Novo Nordisk convenes annually with all the animal-welfare groups in Denmark, to air concerns and set new goals. Every two years, the company invites groups outside Denmark to tour its labs, and it solicits their feedback.

. . . *studies the cultural landscape.* Novo's team of trend-spotters continually tracks news articles on the pharmaceutical industry, activists' campaigns, changes in society's values and expectations of business, and the actions of other pharmaceuticals. It maintains a dynamic "List of Concerns" on bio banks, stem-cell research, gene therapy, and other potentially charged issues, and it issues an internal quarterly report on each. Should an issue arise that might threaten the company's reputation, the trend team quickly alerts upper management.

. . . *publicly holds people accountable.* On its Web site, Novo Nordisk publishes the names and the email addresses of the executive managers who have overall responsibility for bioethics issues.

. . . understands that as it becomes more transparent, the demands for transparency increase. Broadly speaking, society has moved from wanting to *know* a company's activities to wanting to *see* its activities to wanting a *say* in its decision making. Novo has kept pace with that trend, in efforts ranging from the production of a documentary video, *For Whose Sake?*—which provides an unflinching look at animal testing—to engaging in stakeholder dialogues and partnerships. Coming next: an alliance with groups that are exploring alternatives to testing with nonhuman primates in toxicology studies.

Novo Nordisk might not be the best at meeting the transparency imperative. We'll leave that judgment to others. But the company does demonstrate that it's possible for a big global business to let some sunlight in and live to tell about it. "At first, living without curtains feels really uncomfortable," says Holst. "But with time, you become accustomed to the notion that your actions are completely visible to the outside world."

Audit Your Impacts

Transparency depends on data. A company can't reveal its impact on society and the environment without first auditing its social and environmental performance. To assess even one impact, such as greenhouse-gas emissions, a global corporation must trace the emissions of hundreds of suppliers that often are scattered across dozens of countries. Why do it? Because sleuthing the supply chain's carbon output can yield startling insights, as Timberland, for one, has discovered. Insight is the precursor to innovation, and it anticipates the near-certainty that environmental impacts, like carbon emissions, will soon become a direct financial expense.

To calculate the amount of carbon dioxide released in creating its boots, Timberland chased down both its greenhouse-gas emissions and those of its suppliers. Going in, the company predicted that shipping its footwear and apparel from factories to stores would account for the vast majority of its CO_2 output. Wrong. In fact, it accounted for less than 5 percent.

The real culprit, as Swartz puts it, is "cows in the field." Grass-munching cows emit staggering amounts of methane, which converts to CO_2 in the atmosphere. The result: 90 percent of Timberland's greenhouse-gas output comes from cows and from converting their hide to leather. Which raises a question: is Timberland a cow company or a boot company? In terms of holding itself accountable for its climate impact, the answer clearly is, a cow company. Because the leather accounts for roughly 7 percent of the overall value of the cow, Timberland takes responsibility for 7 percent of the cow's greenhouse-gas emissions.

"This knowledge that we accumulated, in an effort to be transparent around our impacts on the environment, revealed something that we could never have imagined," says Swartz. "To be a more sustainable company, we need to innovate around the cows. We need to find ways to use less leather and still produce a boot that sells."

The same logic applies to transparency. To be a more transparent company, you need to reveal the data that matters. And in Timberland's case, the emissions that matter most don't come out of the tailpipe. They come from just under the tail.

Be an Industry Leader

Up until several years ago, no U.S. company would dream of listing on its Web site its contract factories in developing countries. But when Nike, Gap, and Timberland broke that taboo, it became an issue that every company with a global supply chain needed to think about. Now Timberland is quietly seeking to have a similar impact on the way companies make and sell their footwear. Timberland's tool for change is the Green Index tag, about half the size of a baseball card, that's displayed on many of its shoeboxes.

The Green Index is a marvel of minimalism. Timberland streamlined its sprawling environmental audit to create a label that assesses, on a scale of 0 (best) to 10 (worst), each pair of shoes' impact on climate change, as well as the resources and chemicals used to make them. The Green Index gives consumers a quick, accessible take on key elements of the product's sustainability performance—the good and the bad.

But for Swartz, the consumer is a bit of a proxy. His real goal is to use transparency—upfront information on a product's environmental toll—to prod other companies (and their suppliers) to increase their own transparency, reduce their impacts, and innovate for sustainability.

Swartz explains it this way: "When we say 13 percent of our energy is renewable, we're admitting that 87 percent of our energy isn't. So how does that compare to Nike? The only way to know is for us to put that information on a label, and if consumers decide it's important, Nike will have to tell them.

"Nike is a very competitive company," Swartz continues. "It won't want to disclose its energy from renewables unless it's at least 1 percent better than Timberland. And if Nike gets to 14 percent, we won't have a problem as long as we get to 15 percent. In other words, transparency is a powerful, market-forcing mechanism that can push all of us to act more sustainably."

Clearly, Timberland is attempting to exert its gravitational pull on its universe of competitors, to push them to push the envelope on sustainability. And apparently it's having an effect. Not long after our meetings with Timberland, Wal-Mart unveiled a sweeping plan to have its suppliers "calculate and disclose the full environmental costs of making [the retailer's] products."[24] Wal-Mart intends to distill suppliers' data into a "sustainability index" that consumers can use to compare the environmental footprint of its products. Wal-Mart didn't credit Timberland, of course, and it could take several years to develop a ratings system. But no matter. Wal-Mart understands that greater transparency leads to greater accountability. Already, its hundred thousand suppliers are getting the message.

Companies like Timberland, Novo Nordisk, and Patagonia have seen that the accelerating power of viral media has overridden the carefully scripted, infomercialized communications still venerated by many in the business establishment. These pioneers realize the size of the challenge—to confront the relentless, Internet-powered scrutiny by outsiders of their business activities. Nor do they underestimate the difficulty of the undertaking: to strip away the layers of secrecy surrounding an organization's impacts on society and the environment. They are driven by the paradoxical notion that keeping fewer secrets generates greater trust—that in our bottom-up media culture, trust accrues to the most transparent.

AUTHENTICALLY GOOD

5

BUILDING THE MISSION INTO EVERY PART OF THE BUSINESS

The commercial for the Chevrolet Volt that ran in 2008 was simultaneously innocuous and disingenuous. There was the requisite eco-imagery of blue sky, cute kids, and a sprawling green field surrounding the Volt—a plug-in hybrid sedan—which the ad promised would go up to forty miles "without a drop of gas." As the announcer put it, Chevy has gone from "gas friendly to gas free."[1]

But the small print that flashed at the end of the ad captured the Volt's true distinctiveness: "Not yet available for sale."

That's right. General Motors was using real ads and spending real money to promote a nonexistent product. The car's make-or-break battery technology had not been fully developed; back then, GM merely *hoped* to start mass production by late 2010. It would have been a boon for the environment—and for the U.S. auto industry—if the hybrid had made it into showrooms when GM began hyping its great green hope. But in 2008, the Volt was far more concept than car.

So why did GM shift its buzz machine into overdrive—kicking out ads, PR releases, and keynote speeches with ever-growing fervor—for a hybrid that no one could buy? Well, it wasn't about the car. It was about the company. At a time when fuel-sucking SUVs had helped drive the U.S. auto industry into a ditch, GM was hoping that its phantom Volt would give it a pristine green sheen.

GM is hardly the only big company to have wrapped itself in the mantle of green goodliness while engaging in practices that are arguably less than earth friendly. Toyota rode the Prius to green ascendancy, even as it launched the hulking, V–8-powered Tundra and, in 2007, joined a lobbying group in opposing an increase in federal fuel economy standards.[2]

GM's and Toyota's sleight of hand is a sure sign that the companies can't consistently handle authenticity. And that's a serious dilemma for any company that endeavors to be genuinely sustainable. As John Grant declared in *The New Marketing Manifesto,* "Authenticity is the benchmark against which all brands are now judged."[3]

When so much of what we see and hear is mechanized, digitized, and designed for consumption, authenticity becomes an invaluable attribute. In a world that's populated with spin zones and Disneyfied experiences, we long for the genuine article—even though we often can't define it. *The Daily Show with Jon Stewart,* with its mock newscasts, feels real largely because it unabashedly declares itself a counterfeit. Despite the apparent contradiction, the desire for the authentic remains.

In his book *Authenticity: Brands, Fakes, Spin, and the Lust for Real Life,*[4] David Boyle argues that our hunger for the real deal can be found in the "growth of micro-breweries . . . Fair Trade coffee . . . and of 'real food'—maybe organic—that tastes of something."[5] In *Authenticity: What Consumers Really Want,* James H. Gilmore and B. Joseph Pine II flatly assert: "Practically *all* consumers desire authenticity."[6] And then there's that canny commentator Smokey Robinson, who once opined that whatever the experience, we want it "really, really real."

Or at least, we want it honest. GM, which spent years pitching a "gas free" vehicle at a time when no one could buy it, violated one of authenticity's core principles: integrity. Authenticity comes when a brand does what it says it will do. There's no daylight between the story that the brand tells through its actions and the story that it tells through its words. It's unassuming when it delivers the good news and unvarnished when it reveals the bad. Only then do consumers and stakeholders begin to conclude that the company walks its talk.

Unfortunately, far too many companies that claim to be "responsible" are found wanting when reckoning with the truth. We've already seen how TerraChoice Environmental Marketing, in its 2009 review of more than 2,200 products sold in North America, found that 98 percent committed some variety of greenwashing.[7] Our own informal review of the many cases of greenwashing over the past few years yielded four archetypal green pretenders.

- *The Shape Shifter:* Greens its image without changing its essence.

Case in point: BP used its "Beyond Petroleum" ad campaign to bolster its green credentials and highlight its comparatively modest spending on renewable energy (less than 1.5 percent of its budget on solar power), while it continued to make mega-investments in oil and natural gas. But the oil titan's high-profile rhetoric failed to square with images of its enormous 2006 spill on Alaska's North Slope and its scarring of a vast wilderness landscape to extract crude from Canada's tar sands. Not surprisingly, a backlash soon followed. (To cite just one example, activists described tar-sands oil extraction as "one of the world's greatest environmental crimes."[8]) By the spring of 2009, the colossus announced that safety was now its "number one priority," which led some environmental groups to conclude that the company was retreating to its all-petrol roots. Inevitably, more than a few wags suggested that BP should henceforth stand for "Back to Petroleum."

- *The Propagandist:* Blunts genuine bad news with fake good news.

Case in point: In May 2009, when *60 Minutes* aired a lacerating report on oil company pollution in Ecuador's rain forest, Chevron countered with its own self-flattering video, in which it tried to deflect accusations that its subsidiary, Texaco, was responsible for the mess. As the *New York Times* pointed out, Chevron used many of the techniques of credible, independent journalism to produce a "report" that neglected to inform viewers that they were watching a corporate-sponsored advocacy piece.[9] Some might write off Chevron's sham story as bare-knuckled PR, but given its clear lack of integrity, the segment came off as simply knuckleheaded. As of this writing, it had drawn fewer than five thousand views on YouTube. Still, that paltry number didn't keep Chevron from bragging that it had used an "award-winning journalist" to present a "factual story."

• *The Incrementalist:* Hypes narrow, eco-friendly efforts without changing its core, eco-unfriendly business.

Case in point: Most quasi-green companies are not quite so cloddish as Chevron. The Clorox Company has done an impressive job of adding an earth-friendly luster to its image by nabbing earthy Burt's Bees and launching the GreenWorks line of natural cleaners. But despite its best efforts at cleansing its image, Clorox can't quite conceal the fact that at its core it's still a big-time bleach company. Take, for example, a series of ads that the bleach maker ran in early 2009 for its amped-to-the-max cleaner Formula 409. Clorox boasted that it had the desire and the capacity to develop an even brawnier product, Formula 410, "but it would be illegal in twelve states." The ad implied that if Clorox reformulated 409 just one more time, environmental regulators would ban the chemical-laced product. Perhaps Clorox's true color is not quite as green as it would like us to believe.

• *The Double-Talker:* Puts serious marketing and R&D muscle into environmentally sustainable initiatives, even as it continues to profit from pollution and undermine efforts to pass environmentally beneficial legislation.

Case in point: In 2005, General Electric launched "Ecomagination," an ambitious effort to develop products and services that deliver a sustainability improvement of at least 10 percent. Like most such initiatives,

Ecomagination is partly a corporate-imaging effort. It's also very real. By late 2008, GE's R&D investment in cleaner technologies had climbed to more than $2.5 billion; as of this writing, the conglomerate aims to sell north of $20 billion worth of "environmentally friendly" products. There's just one problem: GE's actions haven't always lived up to its rhetoric. For example, in 2007, even as GE flaunted Ecomagination, it worked behind the scenes to get the federal Environmental Protection Agency to weaken its antismog rules for locomotives.[10]

Despite chairman and CEO Jeffrey Immelt's pledge to make GE one of the world's foremost combatants of climate change, the company's backdoor lobbying undermines its credibility. Yes, GE has put serious R&D resources into "solving today's environmental problems." But when it joins with Caterpillar and Alcoa to bolster an industry trade group in its fight against mandatory cuts in greenhouse gases, as it did in 2008, it's safe to conclude that GE has dipped at least a bit of its brand in greenwash.[11]

ANOTHER INCONVENIENT TRUTH

Make no mistake: to varying degrees, *all* companies are environmentally destructive, and most are probably socially destructive as well. On a net basis, virtually every company takes more from the Earth than it returns; as a result, the planet is worse off. Given that every organization is to some degree imperfect, it's vital that companies be transparent about their social and environmental shortcomings as well as their successes. Unfortunately, too many companies are unwilling to acknowledge their failings, and too many attempt to assume a green guise that they haven't earned.

In their race to embrace a sustainable ethos, GE, Clorox, Toyota, BP, and many others have emitted that heat-trapping gas called hypocrisy. They are not alone. Despite the surging interest in conscientious capitalism, there remains a yawning gap between what companies say they value and what they actually do.

A 2007 report by the Boston College Center for Corporate Citizenship, aptly titled "Time to Get Real: Closing the Gap Between

Rhetoric and Reality," found that 60 percent of surveyed executives claim that corporate citizenship plays into their business strategy to a "large or very great extent."[12] Problem is, just 39 percent assert that sustainability is part of their business planning process—and only 25 percent have a team that's responsible for citizenship issues. There's more. Seventy-six percent of executives say corporate citizenship fits their companies' traditions and values, but just 36 percent talk to their employees about it. Bradley Googins, the center's executive director, reported that the credibility gap is now so pervasive, it's become an (unacceptable) "status quo."

Greenwashing scouts speak of the "hidden tradeoff," whereby a single environmental attribute, rather than a holistic set of characteristics, is used to assert that a product is "green." But with many aspiring green giants, the hidden tradeoff applies to the company, not just the product. They use the promise of a single breakthrough innovation (GM's Volt or Clorox's GreenWorks) or the badge from a narrow cluster of environmental good deeds (BP's and GE's alternative-energy efforts) to give their companies a greener luster than they actually deserve.

The hidden tradeoff is not just a marketing gimmick. It is symptomatic of a company's difficult journey toward becoming a new kind of organization. Quite often, companies that aspire to do good, but haven't fully achieved that goal, make do-gooding claims that fail to match their actions. The one sure way for companies to actually walk their talk is to put the goal of serving a larger purpose at the center of their DNA.

PUTTING SUSTAINABILITY AT THE CORE

Skeptics dismiss the notion that companies can truly build sustainability into the core of their operations, so that it influences decisions across the organization. Based on the evidence to date, the skeptics have a point. As Michael Porter and Mark Kramer wrote in a groundbreaking 2006 *Harvard Business Review* article, despite CEOs' avowed commitment to "corporate responsibility," in most cases their efforts remain "too unfocused, too shotgun, too many supporting someone's pet project with no real connection to the business."[13]

And yet, as Porter and Kramer acknowledge, if combining for-profit moneymaking with a for-benefit mission is approached in a strategic way, it can become part of a company's competitive advantage. There's really no other choice. *Any* company that declares itself to be "sustainable" had better put that goal at the center of its growth strategy. If the words are merely a marketing pitch, consumers will quickly sense that the company is just a poser, and a torrent of rebuke will soon follow. When a giant such as BP attempts to green up its image with some feel-good advertising, without fundamentally changing its business, it risks breeding consumer cynicism toward companies that are genuinely trying to do good.

Rather than an end in itself, authentically melding sustainability with strategy really is a journey, and a challenging one at that. Very few profit-making enterprises have pushed sustainability into all of their business activities. None have been able to fully make all business activities sustainable. However, some notable pioneers are taking on the hard work of reinventing their cultures and altering the corporate mindset. They understand that both the promise and the peril of "making it real" are, indeed, very real.

Unfortunately, there's no recipe for originality; each brand must build its own primary source code. But good companies, which stand on values that emotionally connect with consumers, draw on five attributes that give rise to authenticity. We've already seen how Patagonia, the iconoclastic outdoor gear and apparel maker, has set the bar for radical transparency. Equally impressively, Patagonia embodies each of the attributes that fuel authenticity.

A BLUEPRINT FOR AN AUTHENTICALLY SUSTAINABLE BUSINESS: PATAGONIA

Is Patagonia the world's most authentic brand? Nicholas Ind, author of *Living the Brand,* makes a persuasive case that the answer is an unequivocal yes. "The word 'authentic,'" asserts Ind in an online interview, "somehow encapsulates exactly what is impressive about Patagonia."[14] Ind cites employees' vivid connection with the company's mission and values as compelling evidence that Patagonia is the epitome of a genuinely sustainable brand and a model for every company that wants to put its purpose at the center of its profit-making. Many other commentators have likewise argued that in terms of its ability to weave environmental and social sustainability into the fabric of its business, Patagonia stands apart.[15] Here's how Patagonia keeps things real.

Have a Clear Point of View.

Visitors to Patagonia's headquarters in Ventura, find the following words inscribed on the front door: "There is no business to be done on a dead planet." This in-your-face quote, from the Sierra Club's first executive director, David Brower, is pure Patagonia. The words are uncompromising in their assertion that the world is in the midst of an environmental crisis. Business's foremost responsibility, the quotation implies, is not to shareholders, customers, or employees, but to the planet itself. It's tough to be ambivalent and still be authentic; Patagonia's lasting resonance is due in large part to its unsubtle, unwavering commitment to environmental stewardship and sustainability.

Serve a Larger Purpose.

If a brand can convincingly argue that its profit-making is a by-product of its pursuit of a larger purpose, authenticity arises. Patagonia's chief ambition, "[to] use business to inspire and implement solutions to the environmental crisis," is vividly articulated in its mission statement, which makes no mention of profit. Yes, profit matters—but only as evidence that consumers approve of Patagonia's performance, and only as a signal that the company is a leader worth emulating. As Patagonia cofounder Yvon Chouinard has written, "No company will respect us . . . if we are not profitable."[16]

Be Your Own Best Customer.

Can authenticity be simulated? Marketing mavens who try to "think like the customer" would have us believe so. Patagonians, however, have no need for such experiments—they *are* the customer. They are part of the same athletic, adventurous, zealous tribe that buys the company's gear and subscribes to its ethos of aggressively protecting the world's wild places.

Anyone who doubts this need only spend a few minutes with Patagonia's receptionist, Chip Bell, an eleven-time world Frisbee champion who's steeped in the organization's values. Brand strategist Nicholas Ind notes that Bell, like most of Patagonia's associates, has a workplace persona that "has not been defined through a corporate rulebook, but rather because he identifies with Patagonia's deeper purpose."[17] Unlike conventional companies, Patagonia has never had to alter its culture to be "responsible" or "sustainable"; from the beginning, it hired people like Bell—genuine "dirtbags" who are more at home at a base camp than a desk, but who also have a strong affinity for the company's mission. At Patagonia, there is little daylight between the consumer and the employee, or the company and the cause.

Have an Image That's Rooted in the Backstory.

"At the heart of the Patagonia image," writes Chouinard, "is our origin as a blacksmith shop."[18] The company traces its roots to the mid-1960s and the Chouinard Equipment Company, a funky band of alpinists who crafted some of the world's finest climbing tools. In 1972, when they branched into clothing, Chouinard and his crew formed a new company called Patagonia.

Though the decades have rolled by, the past is never far from the present. The metal shed where the ironmongers plied their trade stands catty-corner to Patagonia's main headquarters. And the beliefs and attitudes of the independent, antiauthoritarian climbers who worked the anvils at Chouinard Equipment have forged Patagonia's modern-day image, which consists of a hard-core commitment to building high-quality hardware—and to reveling in the world's wildest places. Patagonia stays authentic by living up to its past.

Practice Integrity.

When a truly responsible company unabashedly concedes its social and environmental shortcomings, it begins to gain an authentic mien. Over its nearly forty-year history, Patagonia has earned a slew of green merit badges. As we noted in the previous chapter, the company committed to using only organic cotton when there was no reliable supply—and the increased costs might well have sunk sales. It was also the first outdoor apparel maker to convert its line of fleece jackets to a feedstock that uses recycled PET bottles, it was the first to recycle polyester apparel into entirely new clothes, it annually donates 1 percent of its sales (not profits) to scores of grassroots environmental organizations, and it has set itself up as a tool for positive social change. Yet at no time has Patagonia claimed that it is "sustainable" or even especially "responsible." In its mission statement, Patagonia pledges to "do no *unnecessary* harm" [emphasis added]. The wording is deliberate. The company avoids promising "no harm" or even "least harm" because in its view those are unachievable standards.

"There's no such thing as sustainable manufacturing," says Patagonia's chief of environmental initiatives, Rick Ridgeway. "It just doesn't exist. The flip side of 'no unnecessary harm' is our recognition of the fact that many of our activities are harmful."[19]

Of course, recent efforts to innovate in the practice of "cradle-to-cradle" and "closed-loop" manufacturing, whereby the resources used in production are designed to be recaptured and "upcycled" into environmentally superior products, may someday prove Ridgeway wrong. But his underlying argument is irrefutable. Patagonia is believable because it recognizes that its contributions to waste and pollution are part of the problem. The company's environmental good deeds are a kind of "penance for our sins," says Ridgeway. That frank admission lends credence to Patagonia's story and ensures that Patagonia's journey toward total sustainability, although probably unattainable, starts from a genuine place.

IS AUTHENTICITY INCOMPATIBLE WITH GROWTH?

When a company has a healthy disregard for all things formulaic, it's all the more likely that authenticity sets in. Nevertheless, as Patagonia demonstrates, authenticity does depend on at least five practical and nameable principles:

- Stand for something unique.
- Put purpose before profit (knowing that profit will follow).

B CORP.'S ACID TEST FOR AUTHENTICITY

Perhaps there's no surer way for a company to live up to the authentic imperative—to ensure that its actions match its claims—than to become a B Corporation. Launched by three college friends who succeeded as entrepreneurs, B Lab is a Philadelphia-based nonprofit that provides a certification system for companies that want to harness the power of private enterprise to create social benefit. (The "B" stands for the "benefits" created for all stakeholders, not just shareholders.) To become a B Corporation, a company must demonstrate a high standard of social and environmental performance by achieving a high score on the B Impact Rating System, which assesses the company's effect on its employees, suppliers, community, and the environment.

Of greater importance, the company is required to amend its articles of incorporation to say that directors must consider, in addition to the interests of shareholders, the needs of employees, the community, and the environment. In a fundamental sense, B Corporations must reformulate the genetic code of their businesses, to make themselves accountable to *all* stakeholders. "These companies are using the power of markets and the power of entrepreneurship to solve social and environmental problems," Jay Coen Gilbert, a B Lab cofounder, told us. "They want to use business to not only create shareholder value, but to create value for society."

In just its first two years, B Lab certified more than 200 companies in more than 50 industries, from financial-services firms, banks, and high-tech outfits to business-to-business, educational, and telecom companies. (Full disclosure: Seventh Generation is a proud founding B Corp.) With so many companies declaring themselves "responsible" and "environmental," it's tough to tell which are genuine and which are fake. B Lab's performance and legal standards amount to a truth test for distinguishing responsible companies from clever marketing. They also announce to investors and warn potential buyers that the company's values inform all of its strategic decision-making.

An ecosystem is emerging around B Lab's certification standards. They're being used by thousands of companies to benchmark their social and environmental performance (a first step toward becoming a full-fledged B Corp), and by institutional investors to drive capital beyond socially responsible investing to a new asset class of "impact investments"[20] that generate social and environmental value as well as financial return.

In effect, B Lab is building a support system for what some call the "fourth sector" (distinct from the government, business, and nonprofit sectors)—an emerging category of hybrid companies that are driven by both social and financial goals and therefore fall somewhere between conventional companies and philanthropies. Such a company isn't a for-profit, nor is it a not-for-profit. It's what some call a "for-benefit." And unlike many nonprofits, for-benefits have the ability to scale, because they can attract capital.

Coen Gilbert predicts that in a generation, these fourth sector, or for-benefit companies will eventually make up 10 percent of the nation's GDP. Already B Corps amount to a higher standard for any company that aspires to be authentically responsible.

- Build the company around a cause.
- Live up to your past.
- Make your actions match your words.

It all sounds so straightforward, which makes it all the more perplexing that so many companies get wrapped around the axle when they lay claim to being really, really responsible. Patagonia has proven that a bunch of Californian nonconformists can build a genuinely authentic, highly influential enterprise, but this closely held outfit lives free and far from Wall Street's demands. Given the proliferation of greenwashing over the past few years, true authenticity seems elusive at best, especially for publicly traded companies. A comparatively small company might seize on it, but how in the world do you scale such a thing?

Size might not subvert to authenticity, but it often diminishes it. When a brand spreads far beyond its home turf, its branches almost invariably (though not inevitably) weaken. Tom's of Maine and Burt's Bees lost a bit of their authentic, home-grown feel when they were snatched up by the likes of Colgate-Palmolive and Clorox—global behemoths trying to act local.

Yet it doesn't have to be that way for all big brands. A colossus from the Pacific Northwest—Beaverton, Oregon–based Nike—has clearly demonstrated that ubiquity, sustainability, and authenticity can be compatible.

THE USER'S GUIDE TO SCALING AUTHENTICITY: NIKE

With $19.5 billion in annual revenue, a vast supply chain that spans the planet, and a portfolio that takes in almost every product known to sport, Nike is a big American company that more often than not has managed to stay relevant and real. Arguably, few other multinationals have worked as long at becoming authentically responsible as Nike. Since the early 1990s, when activists made it the world's foremost symbol of corporate gluttony and ethical recklessness, Nike has traveled a long, hard road toward instilling an ethos of environmental and social stewardship practices into all of its operations. It's nowhere near to fully succeeding on that front; it continues to attract a small army of detractors. But its progress thus far offers valuable lessons for any company that seeks to travel the same path.

Nike lately has skirted the greenwashing morass by largely avoiding green claims. It has moved from heralding "corporate responsibility" and "codes of conduct" to mining sustainability as a source of innovation. In June 2009, Nike restructured its CR department, better positioning itself to drive sustainability through all of the company's operations. And it gave the team a new name, "Sustainable Business and Innovation," to signal a more ambitious goal: to use sustainability to seize on emerging business opportunities.

"If you're pushing sustainability because you think it will enhance the company's reputation, you'll have a problem with authenticity, because there'll be times when your reality doesn't live up to your rhetoric," Hannah Jones, Nike's sustainability chief, told us. "But if you're into sustainability because you think it will drive innovation, as we think it will, then talking about it almost becomes irrelevant."[21]

Keep Mission and Legacy Front and Center.

Walk up to the front entrance of the McEnroe building on Nike's 177-acre campus, and you will undoubtedly see a large orange banner that bears this inscription: "If you have a body, you're an athlete." The quote is from Bill Bowerman, the legendary University of Oregon track coach and Nike cofounder, who died in 1999. Nike may be closing in on its fifth decade, but its rich heritage remains ever-present.

Bowerman's quote appears just below Nike's mission statement— "To bring inspiration and innovation to every athlete in the world"—which greets employees and visitors as they enter Nike's corporate headquarters. This statement of purpose pops up all around Nike's campus. Although it lacks the emotional wallop of Patagonia's David Brower quote, it nevertheless declares what matters most: inspiring and, more important, *innovating* for the customer/athlete. Nike stays relevant—and therefore authentic—by giving associates and stakeholders a sense of shared destiny.

Elevate Sustainability to the Top of the Corporate Agenda, and Authenticity Follows.

Green pretenders typically rank sustainability goals high in the corporation's communications but low on its strategic priorities. Nike reverses that order. As vice president of sustainable business and innovation, Jones directs a team of 135 people worldwide and reports directly to the chief executive; she also meets with the board of directors' corporate responsibility committee every two months. She connects far more frequently with CEO Mark Parker; her office is just around the corner from his office. The fact that she sits on the same floor as the heads of all of Nike's business units both elevates sustainability's prominence within the organization and ensures that it's hardwired into the company's strategic planning.

Though the term remains part of her title, Jones believes that "corporate responsibility" fails to capture the scope of her work. She devotes far more of her focus to using sustainability to spark innovation (she calls her unit "an innovation team") and regularly references the notion of "return on investment squared": to shareholders and to Nike's universe of stakeholders. "We can do well and do good at the same time," she says. "When we see an opportunity to cut waste and also save money in the margin, we elevate it."

In 2006, for example, an internal study showed that Nike was spending $800 million a year on materials that never made it into consumers' closets, from catalogs and point-of-purchase displays to samples and factory scraps. According to Nike's own definition, 42 percent of everything it produced was waste. By innovating ways to reuse materials, cut marketing collateral, and reduce packaging, Jones's team conserved landfill space and saved millions. Just as important, the team signaled to CR skeptics within Nike that thinking sustainably could yield positive bottom-line results.

"In the past, corporate responsibility was more about managing risk and reputation," she says. "But we've moved closer to working at the core of the business model. We're more like consultants to the business units. And if you're going to be a credible consultant at Nike, you'd better bring real business acumen to the table."

Persist Through Setbacks to Build Authenticity.
Despite the hyperattentiveness to innovation, the effort to improve working conditions in Nike's contract factories—part of a global supply chain that employs nearly eight hundred thousand workers in fifty-two countries—has been an arduous process marked by setbacks. In an insightful article for the *Harvard Business Review*,[22] Simon Zadek, managing partner of AccountAbility, a London-based consultancy, demonstrated that Nike's journey has taken it through five major evolutionary phases, which saw it gain credibility by persevering through reversals. In our view, three phases are especially relevant to the larger quest to stay authentic.

Phase One: Reluctant compliance. In the early 1990s, when disclosures of appalling abuses (like child labor) in some of its suppliers' factories sparked protests and boycotts, Nike reacted defensively. The world's largest footwear company was targeted partly because of the ubiquity of its iconic swoosh, which was assertively declared by Nike to stand for quality products and a company worthy of respect. At the time, as Zadek observes, Nike's poor oversight of its factories was no worse than that of its competitors. But no matter. Bowing to pressure from activists, Nike drew up codes of conduct and hired high-profile firms to audit the factories. But labor groups questioned the firms' independence and quickly challenged the results—as well as Nike's credibility.

Phase Two: Go professional. In 1998, Nike established a Corporate Responsibility department, "acknowledging that acting responsibly . . . was an aspect of business that had to be managed like any other." Despite assembling a CR team that grew to more than eighty professionals, reports of abuses in Nike's factories continued to flare. An exhaustive study later showed that Nike's own business practices, such as mandating tight product-delivery deadlines that drove up overtime, were helping to fuel violations of the very labor codes that Nike itself had established. Only then did Nike understand that it had to "manage corporate responsibility as a core part of the business."

Phase Three: Push for "collective responsibility." Early in the last decade, Nike openly declared that it couldn't go it alone. To truly reform its suppliers' factories, it would have to engage its entire industry, as well as policymakers. In 2000, Nike cofounder Phil Knight announced the company's "support of global standards for social auditing" and called on every apparel maker to measure its performance against those standards. Knight calculated, writes Zadek, that when the "social performance records of all the companies were made public . . . Nike would be revealed as a leader." That has largely proved to be the case, as Nike has "moved from a target of attack to a convener of erstwhile critics" on issues involving the welfare of garment-factory workers in developing countries.

Yet for all of Nike's hard-won success in keeping pace with the public's evolving expectations of what it means to be "responsible," the evidence suggests that the working conditions in its factories have largely failed to improve. Richard Locke, a professor at MIT's Sloan School of Management, spent many months poring over Nike's audit data; in 2006, he released his findings. They weren't pretty. Despite "significant efforts and investments by Nike...workplace conditions in almost 80 percent of its suppliers have either remained the same or worsened over time."[23]

The reasons range from weak government regulations in emerging economies—which leaves it up to the brands to police their suppliers there—to the fact that Nike has limited leverage at factories where its contracts are seasonal and therefore short-term. But in a way, the causes didn't matter nearly so much as the report's implicit message: by itself, monitoring wasn't working.

We thought Nike would slam Locke's damning report, but we were wrong. "I loved [the report]," exclaimed Jones. "It was a wakeup call to the industry and our stakeholders, that it's time to change our approach. Policing isn't going to solve it. We need to reboot the entire system."

Nike hasn't backed off from auditing factories, but it has embraced an additional approach: instead of simply monitoring workers, it's empowering them. Nike has begun to champion lean manufacturing, which organizes workers into multitasking teams—and therefore requires more self-management and a greater degree of flexibility and cooperation among workers. That, in turn, should put upward pressure on the factories' management to improve wages and conditions so as to retain high-skilled labor. Or at least that's the theory. Predicts Jones: "When management sees how much value-added the workers deliver, management will start to value them in a better way."

Nike has established a lean manufacturing training center in Vietnam, where it educates managers from long-term suppliers on how to build progressive HR practices and push decision making to the front lines. And it has given itself a hard deadline: by 2011, the company aims to eradicate "excessive overtime" in all of its suppliers' factories. In the meantime, Nike's determination to keeping working the problem, even after nearly two decades of setbacks and not nearly enough successes, has earned it a hard-won measure of credibility. As Zadek and other commentators have observed, Nike has evolved from being an object of activists' scorn to becoming a key leader in civil efforts to make manufacturing in the developing world more humane.

"Get Real" by Taking a Cold-Eyed Look at the Size of the Challenge.

Nike's long slog on the road to improving conditions in its contract factories, combined with some early but limited successes in recycling and green chemistry, led it to conclude that incremental change is a woefully inadequate response to the environmental and social problems that all companies face. As Jones recalls, Parker issued a challenge to Nike's sustainability team: "Put the sustainability ethos at the heart of what we do, which is innovation and design. Make our products live and breathe sustainability."

Parker's sense of urgency grew from compelling evidence that in the not-so-distant future, government mandates and consumer demands will force business to account for many of the external costs that it has so far efficiently avoided. Nike anticipates that it will soon have to reckon with a swarm of unnerving challenges: water rates will skyrocket as the availability of clean water declines, manufacturers will be taxed on the carbon they emit, and legislation will require companies to take their products back at the end of their useful lives and refurbish them into new products. Companies that continue to follow a "business as usual" path will have less room to maneuver and a greater likelihood of failure. Given these new realities, the goal of Nike's sustainability team is to act as advance scouts who will lead the company into the Green Economy.

"Our biggest innovation challenge," says Jones, "is to create new business models that make us a truly sustainable company and prepare us for a radically different business environment."

Create an Authentically Responsible Company by Letting Individuals "Own" Sustainability.

Parker and Jones determined that the CR team needed to work at the beginning of the innovation pipeline, where strategy is set and creativity occurs, rather than at the end, where outcomes are audited and after-action CR reports are filed. The way to accomplish this, Jones believes, is to stop thinking about sustainability as a compliance or risk-management function. She wants her team to act as an idea lab that pushes innovation, but at the same time allows business units to "own" sustainability and include it in their day-to-day work.

How do you plant the seeds of sustainability and help others harvest them? Nike's "Considered" team offers a model. It's an "in-house sustainability think tank" that is tackling knotty challenges—cutting pollutants and waste, conserving energy and water, and adding ecologically beneficial materials—by yoking the creative power of the company's designers. They are the innovators responsible for fashioning the next generation of Nike gear, and they make hundreds of daily decisions that ripple across thousands of products—and ultimately determine the size of Nike's environmental footprint. So the think tank has created a predictive tool that quantifies, in real time, the ecological impact of each and every one of the designers' choices: it's a desktop program called the Considered Index (hence the team name).

When designers sketch a new running shoe, they log the specs into the Considered Index, which crunches an overall score based on how well the prototype measures against a myriad of tests, such as the percentage of toxic solvents, natural materials, and recycled waste. As the model moves toward final design, the index highlights where upgrades can be made. In this way, the index helps designers to not only "consider" the environmental consequences of their creations but also improve on them. The index even awards "early adopter" points for designers who take up an environmentally beneficial innovation within its first year of development—a potent catalyst for propagating change. Each design team's Considered score is posted publicly, which fuels internal competition and sparks the conversations that lead to breakthrough innovation.

"The index allows us to make every designer an agent of sustainability," says Lorrie Vogel, who heads the Considered team. "So when they see they get a better score by reducing adhesives, which emit VOCs, they develop snap-together tooling that completely *eliminates* adhesives. The designers chip away at our overall environmental impact, one decision at a time."

Achieve Authenticity by Asking Different Questions.

Ask businesspeople for their company's gross margins and profitability, and more often than not you'll get an immediate answer. But ask how much water and energy the company consumes or how much waste it produces, and almost always you'll get blank stares. A company can't be authentically sustainable if it doesn't fill in the blanks. That's what Nike sought to accomplish when it created the Considered Index.

Hunting down answers to difficult questions often requires months of tough, investigative scut work—exactly what a team of Considered sleuths endured when they set out to build the sprawling database that underlies the index. Nike charged the team of intrepid investigators with uncovering the chemical composition and environmental impacts of the raw materials and the manufacturing processes used by the company. The gumshoes traveled to factories in China and elsewhere and collected samples of rubber, leather, nylon, polyester, foams, and more.

Back in the lab, the team deconstructed each material to determine its chemical composition. They then quantitatively evaluated and ranked the material according to a sweeping range of impacts arrayed across four categories: chemistry (carcinogens, acute and chronic hazards, and endocrine disruptors), energy intensity (kilograms of carbon emitted per kilogram of material), water intensity (liters of water consumed per kilogram of material), and physical waste (during manufacture and "end of life" disposal). Each category was then assigned a numeric value, which lets the Considered Index calculate the overall sustainability score of each design.

The team also identified environmentally beneficial materials, which do less harm to the air, land, water, and human health. These "environmentally preferred materials" were then arranged on three platforms: *regenerated* (materials produced with pre- and/or post-consumer recycled content, such as recycled rubber and polyester), *renewable* (raw materials, such as bamboo and organic cotton, that are rapidly replenished after harvest), and *chemically optimized* (materials that cut down on toxic substances, such as organic wool and synthetic leather that uses fewer solvents). Once these preferred materials were entered into the index's database, designers could see how to increase the sustainability quotient across the company's entire product portfolio. In this way, the index gives designers a compelling image of the future that Nike wants to create.

Nike's superstar designer, Tinker Hatfield, delivered tangible evidence of the Considered Index's innovation potential when he fashioned the 2009 evolution of Nike's most celebrated sneaker, the Air Jordan XX3. Hatfield rebuilt the shoe from the ground up, by reimagining it through the lens of sustainability. Among the shoe's many environmental breakthroughs, Hatfield eliminated chemical-based adhesives by interlocking the pieces like a jigsaw puzzle and overlaying them with stitching, which gave the XX3 a radically different look. The XX3 was the first Air Jordan to effectively marry sustainability and performance; Nike estimated it would sell half a million pairs. Just as important, Hatfield inspired other designers to follow his lead and discover new ways to bake sustainability into their creations—one more way that sustainability gets embedded into a company's creative process.

Equally impressive, Hatfield's innovations swayed his biggest skeptic, Michael Jordan himself. "When Tinker told him that he wanted to make the Jordan XX3 sustainable, Jordan was like, 'Not on my watch,'" Jones recalls. "He probably thought 'green' equals 'less.' But Tinker saw it as an innovation challenge. He gave himself a different box of constraints, which forced him to innovate in a different way. When Jordan saw the result, he told Tinker, 'From now on, every Jordan shoe is going to be sustainable.'"

Yet in its marketing of the XX3, Nike played up the shoe's top performance and bold styling, but not so much its "eco-friendliness." Nike reasoned that look and feel matter to the professional athletes who wear the shoe and the millions of kids who emulate them, whereas sustainability carries far less resonance. Even so, the Jordan XX3 is Nike's most environmentally fit basketball shoe, bar none. It set a new design standard for sustainability, but Nike didn't feel compelled to shower the shoe with green praise. Somehow, that feels more authentic.

"We all want to do even more around sustainability—it's absolutely essential to growing the business," says Vogel. "But we don't feel the need to *say* more. The most important thing is that we do the work that needs to be done, and let the result speak for itself."

Follow the North Star.

The Considered Index helps designers make the kind of granular, daily decisions that build toward increasingly higher degrees of sustainability. But the index doesn't give designers and other innovators an overarching picture of what Nike's version of sustainability will look like in the future. So in 2008, in partnership with the non-profit sustainability consultancy Natural Step, Nike developed an additional framework for navigating toward a long-term vision of a sustainable future: it's called "the North Star." As Jim Goddard, the director of Considered Innovation, commented in a case study prepared by the Natural Step, "the North Star is a far off, guiding light that lets us make sure we stay on the right track."[24]

Nike's North Star pictures a company whose every product is fully "closed loop"; that is, it uses the fewest possible materials, and it's assembled in ways that allow it to be readily disassembled and recycled into new products. The company has already achieved a rough beta version of such a closed loop, through its Reuse-A-Shoe program, which takes worn-out sneakers and turns them into Nike Grind, a material for sports surfaces. The North Star builds on that foundation by helping designers focus more on using materials that are easily recyclable and on innovating in the area of design for disassembly. In this way, the North Star shows designers where Nike wants to someday be and builds clear signposts for navigating the journey. "Because we have a real consensus around our future state," says Vogel, "we believe we'll get there faster."

Let's recap Nike's hard-won lessons for building organizations that are authentically sustainable:

- Tell your story, over and over again, to employees and stakeholders alike.
- Put sustainability at the top of the food chain.
- Make your goals explicit.
- Push through defeat—battle scars are badges.

- Create a real-world picture of your biggest challenges.
- Build tools that help people "own" sustainability.
- Ask different questions—and put in the sweat equity to discover better answers.
- Set your compass to True North.

Heed these lessons, and instead of trying to make claims based on a narrow set of do-good deeds, you'll have helped create a responsible company that really is "really real." Better yet, you'll be confident enough not to have to brag about it.

THE COOPERATIVE COMPANY 6

BUILDING PROFITS AND SOLVING PROBLEMS
THROUGH MASS COLLABORATION

It takes all of two minutes to view some resounding evidence that the balance of power is shifting decisively from the company to the consumer. Let us explain.[1]

When Fred Wilharm, a real-estate investor from Franklin, Tennessee, paid off $3,000 on a Lowe's Visa card, he expected the issuers to woo him with another round of rewards programs or at least raise his borrowing limits.[2] Instead, the card companies jacked up his rates. Wilharm was infuriated. Not so long ago, his only recourse would have been to complain to a disinterested bureaucrat at the Better Business Bureau. But with the advent of online social technologies, he found a far more gratifying way to fight back.

In a YouTube video dubbed "The Tennessee Credit Card Massacre," Wilharm sliced, diced, and drilled his Lowe's, Visa, and other cards into dozens of ragged little pieces. The two-minute clip is one among several dozen "plastectomies"[3] —videos of cards being chopped, shredded, shot, and set aflame—that popped up across the Internet when the economy tanked. As more consumers defaulted on debts, card issuers raised rates and slapped on new fees, sparking a YouTube-generated backlash. Other outraged consumers launched Web sites on which burned cardholders could vent, often posting blow-by-blow accounts of their fruitless dealings with the card issuers' tone-deaf customer-service representatives. It didn't take long for the mainstream media to chronicle the outcry and for Congress to pass legislation to reform the credit-card industry.

Companies have long been accustomed to holding sway over consumers. Despite the hype that the customer is king, most companies are more often egocentric than customer-centric. Many regard customers as objects of consumption and mere sales figures on their profit-and-loss statements. As Josh Bernoff and Charlene Li assert in an article for the *MIT Sloan Management Review,* the balance of power has long favored large corporations, which typically devise products, deliver services, and concoct marketing messages based on their judgment of what people will buy, not on people's views of what they need. Too many big companies seem indifferent to people's desires, and too many people are chronically frustrated by their interactions with big companies. "The term 'customer-centric' was mostly just a buzzword," Bernoff and Li declare. "Now, though, many customers are no longer cooperating."[4]

The spate of plastectomies and Web sites featuring credit-card horror stories signals that customers are rebelling and companies are losing their advantage. Perhaps you've seen other evidence, such as the video of the Comcast technician who failed to fix an Atlanta customer's Internet connection and instead took a nap on the poor guy's couch. Word of the one-minute YouTube documentary of the snoozefest, titled "A Comcast Technician Sleeping on My Couch," has spread like kudzu over the Internet, drawing more than 1.3 million views. Maybe you've cheered the YouTube clip of an aggrieved AOL customer battling with a bullheaded service representative, which generated nearly a quarter of a million views. And then there's the South Korean blogger's post of stomach-turning photos, which raced through the blogosphere, of slimy conditions at a supplier of Dunkin' Donuts.[5]

By seizing on the universe of communities that span the Web, customers are profiling indifferent and unresponsive brands in ways that are decidedly unflattering. People are using these technologies to shake off their anonymity, assert their individuality, and redefine the typical company-consumer exchange. They desire relationships instead of transactions, authenticity instead of hyperbole. Shoshana Zuboff and James Maxmin, in their superb book *The Support Economy,* put it this way: "[consumers] want to 'opt in' and make their own choices, controlling their destinies and their cash."[6] If they can't get what they need from companies, they pursue it in some online community.

The lesson for leaders of companies that seek to be both responsible and responsive: some smart organizations are engaging in a kind of strategic judo. By inviting consumers to help cocreate their future, they are cultivating people power by giving up (some) control.[7]

SOCIAL TECHNOLOGIES FOR THE SOCIAL GOOD

We've seen how the open-source software movement dramatically demonstrated that by releasing some of the basic building blocks for innovation—in this case, the source code—it could mobilize the total IQ of thousands of individuals from across the Internet. Their volunteerism, fueled by the Web, gave rise to Linux, Mozilla, and the like. We know well the story of how a generation of Web 2.0 companies—YouTube, Facebook, Flickr—tapped into a seemingly bottomless reservoir of creativity by encouraging the masses (not just coders) to contribute to an online product or service. What's new is found in one of the core characteristics that sets these technologies apart from those of the Internet's first generation: their canny way of turning self-interest into social benefit.

By leveraging social technologies, responsible companies are turning consumers into contributors. They are using the Web to engage consumers in honest and transparent conversations. Through all their talking, blogging, and tweeting, innovators and consumers are leveraging the benefits of four of the core design characteristics of good companies:

• Responsible companies don't screen out consumer's views; social networking amounts to a powerful way for companies to demonstrate that *they're listening*. One unlikely example is "Open for Discussion," McDonald's "corporate social responsibility" blog. True, the site issues a view of sustainability that's framed by the Golden Arches. And it sometimes generates more smoke than fire, by occasionally reverting to PR-speak when critics chime in. But it's a solid first step toward demonstrating that Mickey D's is finally willing to publicly engage consumers and critics—and perhaps even to risk seeing itself as we see it.

• When employees use online conversations to talk about what they're working on, it shows that *the company is a community* of creative individuals and not just another monolithic machine. Dell's blog, Direct2Dell, signals that the computer giant is committed to hosting unfiltered, consumer-to-employee conversations on unflattering topics, such as Dell's battery recalls and chronic problems with its overseas call centers. With its unpolished text and video from company tech-heads who want to share news and ideas relating to gadgets and hardware, Direct2Dell humanizes Dell in a way that its wooden founder never could.

• Mission driven companies are *transforming consumers into activists*. Working Assets, the powerful citizen-action group that doubles as a cell-phone and credit-card company,[8] sends 1 percent of each customer's monthly bill and ten cents on each credit-card purchase to a non-profit group that works for human rights and the environment. Thus far, Assets has raised $60 million for progressive causes. But consumers, not some company overlord, vote annually on where the money will go.[9] And the company's CREDO Action Web site provides a virtual village green for people to speak out on causes they believe in. In recent years, Working Assets' network members have sent more than four million messages to legislators, registered more than two hundred thousand new voters, and monitored U.S. polling places to guarantee "free and fair" elections.

Although Working Assets is not a full-fledged open-source company, it has gathered consumers into a movement, one that invites its members to shape the company's mission and direct a portion of its sales. This cooperative company ventures to ask consumers, *How do you want us to do good?*

• Smart companies are also using online conversations to *put consumers at the heart of product innovation.* One such enterprise is Threadless, a T-shirt maker that in 2008 grew its sales by more than 200 percent—even though it lacks operations that were once deemed essential to every business, such as advertising, professional designers, and a sales team. As first reported in a compelling *Inc.* magazine article, Threadless unveils several new lines of T-shirts every month, and it typically sells out every one, largely because it's redefined the logic of production. Since the Industrial Revolution, companies have decided what to make. At Threadless, *consumers* proclaim what the company will make, which vastly increases the likelihood that they will buy the final product.

Threadless runs design competitions through its online community of seven hundred thousand teens and twenty-somethings. Members of the network submit their ideas for T-shirt designs and rate their favorites. A survey by an MIT researcher shows that 95 percent of Threadless customers vote on a design before buying one of its $15 shirts. That democratic approach has helped the company transform passive shoppers into active participants in the R&D process. Says Jeff Lieberman, a Threadless board member, "[We're] a community company that just happens to use T-shirts as a canvas."[10]

Jake Nickell, Threadless's founder and chief strategy officer, describes his cooperative model as just "good common sense." But he and his Threadless cohorts have tapped into something that runs far deeper. Recent evidence from the Max Planck Institute for Evolutionary Anthropology reaffirms that the human species has a remarkable capacity for cooperation.

Seeking to test the notion that human beings are more "generally intelligent" than apes, the institute's researchers administered a battery of "nonverbal IQ tests" to adult chimpanzees and two-year-old children. They found that the kids scored better than their ape counterparts only on those tests that tracked collective social skills: group learning, communicating, and "interpreting the intentions of others." Their conclusion: collective cognition—our ability to invent and to solve problems by cooperating—is what truly sets us apart from other animals. "The great apes communicate almost exclusively for the purpose of getting others to do what they want," writes Michael Tomasello, the institute's codirector, in a *New York Times Magazine* essay describing the experiment. "Human infants, in addition, gesture and talk in order to share information with others—they want to be helpful."[11]

What's true for infants holds true for adults: we are hardwired to create by conferring. Threadless, Facebook, Linux, and their ilk might *seem* different. But in fact, the cooperative company is far more normal—far more *human*—than the conventional company. The cooperative company provokes better insights and ideas because it gives people the chance to collectively ruminate and reflect. Whether it's writing a piece of software code or deciding what social venture to contribute to, the prospect of connecting, competing, and creating with like-minded peers fires people up. The cooperative company speaks authentically to individuals who want their voices to be heard and who want to matter.

The cooperative company is often synonymous with the responsible company. They both replace hierarchy with community, opacity with transparency, assignments with contributions, pure profits with profits for a purpose. Business leaders who are revolutionizing the responsibility ethos are building on the cooperative-company model to cocreate with consumers, thought leaders, and even other companies. We found one of the new pioneers of peer production on Gold Street, in downtown Brooklyn.

THE COMPANY EMBRACES A COMMUNITY: ETSY.COM

Jumpstarted in 2005 by three New York University students headed by Rob Kalin, an entrepreneur and part-time furniture designer, Etsy.com has quickly grown into the eBay of the DIY (do-it-yourself) movement.

Declaring itself as "your place to buy and sell all things handmade," Etsy is a nonstop craft fair featuring bags, candles, "geekery," housewares, quilts, toys, woodwork, and a dizzying universe of other one-off objects. Staffers keep the origins of the company's moniker a mystery, but Etsy certainly sounds like a play on "itsy," as in "itsy-bitsy."[12] Small is a central characteristic of the ethos of craft, which is all about turning out limited batches of handmade goods and selling them on a sustainable scale.

And yet, although it projects the image of a grassroots start-up, Etsy is certainly starting to grow up. Already, it's the largest online marketplace for handmade items, with more than 2.6 million members in 150 countries and nearly 4.3 million listings. Etsy eschews warehouses stuffed full of inventory by providing a platform for sellers to set up online boutiques. And it differs from many Web 2.0 outfits in that it doesn't rely on third-party advertising income. It makes money by charging 20 cents to list an item for four months; by billing crafters up to $15 to highlight their wares on the site's popular Showcase pages; and by taking a 3.5 percent cut on each transaction. That business model helped Etsy triple its gross merchandise sales in the teeth of the 2008 recession, to $90 million, and to set it on a path to more than double such sales in 2009.

Etsy's future, of course, is far from certain. The company was projected to break even for the first time in late 2009; its continued growth depends entirely on the participation and innovation of its sellers. And though it's barely beyond a start-up, Etsy must battle upstart competitors even as it keeps a wary eye on eBay. That said, Etsy's ability to soar when the economy cratered suggests that this is a company that's truly tapped the creative capacity of its community.

Etsy is not your stereotypical do-good enterprise. It doesn't issue a corporate responsibility report. Its funky offline home, six flights up in a drafty rehabbed printing plant, will never qualify as an eco-correct workplace. Its chief executive, Maria Thomas, formerly the head of digital media at NPR, struggles to connect conventional notions of "sustainability" and "green" with Etsy.[13] "Those words are being co-opted by marketers to conjure up a lot of good things, like energy conservation," she told us. "But I don't feel comfortable proclaiming that we're truly sustainable when we're not always living it."[14]

In fact, Etsy *is* living a sustainable ethos, though perhaps not always in terms of watts saved and carbon reduced. Like the Slow Food movement, whose tenets challenge us to recognize "the strong connections between planet and plate,"[15] Etsy's craftspeople, most of them women, often source local "ingredients" to create their wares. Or they'll upcycle discarded materials to fashion something new—and take whatever time they need to do it. Craft itself emphasizes meticulous, mindful practice and skill—an antidote to the frenetic, dehumanizing pace of twenty-first-century life.

Etsy also offers, to its millions of shoppers, an alternative to the ubiquity of chain-store culture. In place of the big-box retailers' conformity and the anonymity of shopping there, Etsy promises self-sufficiency and self-expression. Its first promotional materials, which pictured a kid throwing a rock at a factory, featured the slogan "End mass production." Its updated vision statement is less confrontational but no less ambitious: "To build a new economy and present a better choice: Buy, Sell, and Live Handmade." As Rob Walker asserts in a *New York Times Magazine* piece, Etsy mixes "high minded ideas about consumer responsibility with the unsentimental notion of the profit motive."[16]

Etsy's revenue model depends on people purchasing things—but on its own back-to-the-future terms. It melds Web 2.0 technology with a preindustrial view of commerce, in which the individual buys directly from the maker instead of a big-box retailer. Its response to our throwaway, mass consumer lifestyle is to promote a throwback, craft-based culture in which, as *Wired* proclaims, "the future of shopping is all about the past."[17]

Through a blog, online forums, a wiki, and both physical and online "Labs" where veteran artisans give classes on how to make and sell things, Etsy has built a gathering place for people who want to drop out of the Wal-mart world and take a chance on doing what they love. Etsy is defining a new kind of cooperative model. It's growing revenue and building reputational capital by helping its community of do-it-yourself individualists create a profitable alternative to the Mall. Let's dig into this paragon of a collaborative and responsible company to see what we can learn.

The Company Is the Community

Etsy was launched by and for people like Matthew Stinchcomb, chief wrangler of the Etsy community. Stinchcomb, an ex-art major/professional musician, is part of that drifter generation of creative people in their twenties and thirties—talented folks who are nimble enough and curious enough to try on a variety of different careers. When Rob Kalin launched Etsy, he asked Stinchcomb, with whom he'd run a graphic-design business, to sign on as marketing director. Etsy exudes authenticity largely because it sprang from a globe-spanning range of creative microenterprises like Kalin's and Stinchcomb's—one-person and two-person outfits that were already working independently and wanted to connect.

"We were part of a community of creative professionals who were trying to make a living, and there wasn't a good place for us to sell our work," Stinchcomb recalls. "Etsy was built entirely with artists in mind, and we wanted artists to be involved in the process."

Part of Etsy's ingenuity is that it manages to harness the collective imagination of the sprawling community of crafty folks even as it provides them with platforms to show off their individuality. One of its prime tools for simultaneously harvesting the community's best thinking and spotlighting singular talent is the Treasury, a daily feature that allows any community member to pick a dozen handmade objects from the site's nearly infinite listings and showcase them on a single page. So, for example, an artist who runs a shop called DesignsInFiber curated a Treasury collection of images of trees from different artists, which were rendered in different media—a photograph, oil paintings, quilts, and mosaics. Within a day, the "Beauty in Trees" collection drew an outpouring of comments, all of them positive. (Etsy members can be less than discriminating, but they are highly supportive.) Says CEO Thomas: "We're basically saying that the millions of community members can curate collections faster and with more raw imagination than just a few Etsy employees can."

The Treasury allows an entrepreneur like DesignsInFiber to assume the role of the newspaper editor who chooses what to run on page one. Just as an editor draws more readers to an article by putting it "above the fold," an Etsy curator potentially lures more buyers to a piece of craftwork by featuring it in the Treasury. But although an editor is essentially anointed by senior management and is largely invisible to readers, a curator is self-appointed, highly conspicuous, and easily accessible. Click on the Featured Curator button, and you pull up a page highlighting listings of DesignsInFiber's "knitted home décor," her bio, coordinates for her blog and Twitter sites, and the more than two hundred members who list her shop as a "favorite." Each of Etsy's nearly three million crafters has a story and, through features like the Treasury, the rich means to tell it.

Etsy must not only connect members to the larger community but also bind the community to the company. It stays tightly twined with members largely through the Storque, its intensely interactive, multilayered blog. It's there that staffers post semiregular Works in Progress updates that list accomplishments and lay out priorities for the upcoming months. Etsy's leaders, including Thomas and Stinchcomb, also issue Talking Shop podcasts, where they field top-of-mind questions from community members. Etsy pushes the boundaries of transparency by posting a monthly Weather Report, which unveils sales figures and other vital marketplace statistics (the number of goods sold; pages viewed; new members joined) from the previous thirty days. And then there's Vibe Track, where a full-time associate directly responds to members' postings on Twitter and continually updates Etsy's staff on the community's mood—what's going right and, perhaps more important, what's going wrong.

And make no mistake, things definitely do go wrong. At the time of our interview, Stinchcomb was still smarting over a billing fiasco, in which Etsy changed the minimum amount that sellers must pay on their monthly statements without adequately informing the community. A promised email alert was never sent out and the initiative was launched on a Saturday, when no one was in the office to take calls from confused and angry members.

"The whole community just imploded," he recalls. "At that exact moment, I was speaking at the South by Southwest conference on the importance of transparency and communication. I was praying that no one in the audience was visiting the site, because it was widespread chaos."

The near-disaster propelled Stinchcomb and other leaders to increase the variety of mechanisms that Etsy uses to knit the company with the community. If regular updates, podcasts, and Weather Reports don't always keep community members in the loop, perhaps more management face time in Etsy's user forums will. They believe that the best way for their collaborative company to benefit from the collective genius of its community is to open up even more channels for continuous conversation.

Build Markets for Artisans

Early on, Etsy's founders recognized that the company's success depends on its sellers' success. If the DIY tribes conclude that Etsy is simply profiting from their initiative and inventiveness without brightening their microbrands, they'll quickly abandon the site. For Etsy to grow its business, it must enrich its sellers' businesses. That means helping artisans make their markets, by giving them the tools and technology to entice more qualified buyers than they'd find anywhere else.

So there's a part of Etsy that resembles a real-world business colloquium for indiepreneurs. It holds thrice-weekly online Newbie Chats, where rookies get seasoned advice from staffers and veteran entrepreneurs. The Storque features tutorials on pricing and downloadable spreadsheets for managing inventory. There's also lots of peer-to-peer educating through Etsy Forums, where Etsians discuss the ins and outs of operating a microbusiness (what to do "if a good sale goes bad"), share advice for creating and promoting their work (how to "take great product photos—I may have the answer!"), and critique each other's virtual storefronts. One artisan's invitation to "name one thing that could bring more sales for the shop" drew nearly 1,300 comments—not an unusual number. All in all, Etsy's symposiums are a clever way for the company to train its "suppliers"—the next generation of micromanufacturers.

There's another part of Etsy that resembles a multitiered support group for craft folk, where the company provides the community with tools for engagement. Chief among them is Etsy Teams, an online zone that offers technology, guides, and workshops for the more than five hundred groups of sellers organized around a shared location or craft. Etsy Hookers, to cite one not-so-random example, is a team of several dozen artisans who are passionate about . . . crochet. Building a DIY business may be liberating, but it can also be lonely. Affiliating with a team makes it easier for micromanufacturers to do what people engaged in a kindred endeavor love to do: connect, chat, opine, complain, share, show off, encourage, create, and learn. Etsy has clearly concluded that it must not only spread skills to as many budding entrepreneurs as possible but also encourage and enable relationships amongst as many sellers as imaginable.

Cocreate with the Community

Etsy possesses all the usual WMC (weapons of mass collaboration). It's an online business. It's built around a vast social network. Everything that's sold on Etsy is sourced through the community. But Etsy's most effective weapon is one that every responsible company strives to develop: that fundamental, unflashy core competency called *trust*.

Etsy trusts its community members to manage themselves. There's no overlord who oversees the network, no central command that dictates assignments or curates the site's nearly infinite collection. In fact, the company entrusts its entire business model to its sellers. If artisans don't keep priming Etsy's growth engine with their creativity, the company's sales will tank. Their craft constitutes Etsy's inventory. Members, in turn, trust Etsy to stay true to the community and its values—to do the right thing. Etsy builds trust by striving to be open and accessible. If members want to complain to the company's management, they can easily do so. In addition to such feedback mechanisms as the Storque and Etsy Forums, Stinchcomb and other managers hold weekly online "office hours," in which artisans can ask whatever they want about the site.

"Members are really our partners in this enterprise," says Stinch-comb. "We've always felt that the Etsy brand is really comprised of tens of thousands of micro-brands. We want to grow big by staying small—by keeping our focus on the individual producer."

Etsy is now experimenting with ways to tap into our seemingly unquenchable hunger for the one-of-a-kind. For more than half a generation, we've become accustomed to digital customization: we've TiVo'd our TV entertainment, iPoded our music, and Flickr'd our experiences.[18] We've brought our personalized aesthetic to the physical world as well, by leaving our individual imprint on everything from custom-made watches and cars to PCs and guitars. Etsy is capitalizing on our desire for the unique and the unusual by making it easier for consumers to cocreate directly with crafters. It now runs a service called Alchemy, a feature that allows you to post a request for the novel, bespoke item—a wedding dress, cufflinks, a mustache cup (for real)—and the amount you're willing to pay. Artisans then bid on the opportunity to make what you want and win the sale.

Through Alchemy, Etsy has turned consumers into cocreators. Shoppers treat the site as a kind of creativity commons, where they swap ideas, critique designs, make connections with crafters, and have fun. Most important, they buy. Alchemy frees the company from having to bother with focus groups and market research. Etsy understands that it needn't depend on R&D labs to deliver the best innovations; breakthrough ideas can just as readily come from the people who conceive and then consume the actual product.

Mix Inspiration with Instruction

Meet the Tuckers. You can watch a "Handmade Portraits" video of them at the Storque. Looking like they stepped out of a Grandma Moses painting, Robin and Kathy Tucker live largely off the grid in northern Missouri's hill country. They hand-pump their water and slaughter their own meat from the goats and chickens they raise. Robin is a world-class craftsman who builds lazy Susans and hope chests from diamond-shaped pieces of inlaid Baltic birch, purpleheart, and other exotic wood, which he cuts on a pedal-powered table saw. The couple market their "wood mosaics" via a pair of laptops and a high-speed Internet connection with Etsy and other social networking sites, like MySpace and YouTube. The computers and the outhouse make for a jarring juxtaposition, but they're a natural fit with the Tuckers' digitally driven, back-to-the-land lifestyle. "I could have made more money working in town," says Robin. "But I get more enjoyment making something of beauty."

Etsy's video profile of the Tuckers generated more than seventy comments from the community, whose overall reaction can be summed up in one word: "inspirational!" The Tuckers defiantly demonstrate, in their homespun way, that although it's far from easy, it's still possible to escape the confines of the mainstream working world and live the handmade life. That's what Etsy is selling—freedom as well as craft.

At a time when many companies are cutting salaries, issuing furloughs, and slashing "headcount," Etsy offers creative folks a shot at escaping the uncertainty and conformity of nine-to-five life. That prospect, which underlies the Handmade Portraits videos, is made explicit in the Quit Your Day Job series on the Storque. Day Job hosts daily Q&As with artists like Marcia X of Kahili Creations, whose Etsy-powered jewelry business helped her walk away from her corporate life of "PowerPoint presentations and meetings" and create "the first job I've had that I look forward to every day." The feature is quintessentially Etsian, in that it mixes both the inspirational and the instructive, by delivering models and mentors to help you make the big leap.

Etsy has cleverly positioned itself at the intersection of entrepreneurial passion and practice. It's not an easy place to be. Although Quit Your Day Job proffers the allure of ditching the corporate life, *Fortune Small Business*, quoting an Esty spokesman, reports that the "vast majority of sellers use the site as a 'secondary source of income.'"[19] Although the dream is to make a living at what you love to do, the reality is that the laws of commerce bind even artists. Etsy provides some of the tools and connections to fuel a profitable enterprise, but it's up to sellers to stoke consumer demand.

Despite the aura of chain-store-repudiating self-sufficiency that surrounds Etsy, the company understands that indiepreneurs aren't looking to reject the capitalist system. They just want to put their own iconoclastic stamp on it. If enough of them succeed, perhaps Etsy will realize its stated mission: to "empower people to change the world's economy, one person and one community at a time."

Lay Out Some Lessons

Social networking is, by definition, unpredictable. But chances are, few Web 2.0 companies will live to compete in Web 3.0. Etsy is still a young enterprise, and it may well fall victim to some turbo-charged upstart like ArtFire or DaWanda, or get scooped up by an eBay or an Amazon. Etsy has endured its share of growing pains, including disgruntled sellers who complain of what they describe as poor customer service and a less than user-friendly interface. It's even spawned an anti-Etsy blog, Etsybitch. Still, regardless of what the future holds for Etsy, its evolution offers salient lessons for any enterprise that understands that by collaborating with consumers it becomes authentically responsible—even if it doesn't have a dot-com after its name.

Innovations That Personalize Work Are Magnets for Collaborators and Consumers.

The rise of Etsy has coincided with a return to the tactile. So much of working life consists of laboring at computers and pushing messages across the ether, many of which go unnoticed by all but the intended recipient. Etsy offers an antidote to the anonymity of the electronic workplace. It taps into our innate desire to get our hands dirty and make something that's deeply personal and irrefutably tangible. "Probably a quarter of the people on Etsy aren't even interested in selling," says Stinchcomb. "They just want to show and share what they've made."

The Best Way to Make Connections Is to Tell Stories.

Maria Thomas calls it the "flight to meaningful." Just as stock-market investors flock to "quality" equities during a downturn, people seek out "meaning" in an economic meltdown and the social upheaval that follows. They often find it in the personal connections they make; they often make connections through stories. So it goes with Etsy.

For every "deer cardboard trophy," "reclaimed barn wood American flag," and "Bad Girlz collage" that's featured on Etsy, there's a story—the narrative of its creation and of its creator. People are hungry for objects imbued with the artisan's history and experiences. So at every opportunity—through videos, podcasts, the blog, and more—Etsy gives crafters the opportunity to tell their tales. The video chronicle of Robin and Kathy Tucker's discovery of the DIY life in rural Missouri is *inspirational* to Etsy's sellers, but it's *meaningful* for Etsy's buyers.

To Build the Community, Extend the Conversation.
Etsy resembles a virtual version of Istanbul's Grand Bazaar—a vast, sprawling maze of entrepreneurs who work out of individual stalls, but who know and support one another, even as they compete. Shoppers typically frequent their favorite merchants, and every transaction comes with a conversation. Etsy works relentlessly to build a highly interactive community whose associates, buyers, and sellers can strike alliances, swap ideas, critique creations, share insights, recruit volunteers, barter for a bargain, and keep those conversations growing.

Like the serpentine alleyways that wind through the Grand Bazaar, Etsy's myriad communication pathways make it feel both big and familiar. It's a marketplace that's simultaneously global in its reach and local in the personal connections that it allows. It seems inevitable that by enabling shoppers to connect with makers and hear the stories behind their creations, Etsy will realize another of its ambitions: to get people to think about what they really value and thereby move closer to becoming fully conscious consumers.

THE USER'S GUIDE TO COLLABORATION: IBM

The collaborative-company model is not just for Web 2.0 outfits like Etsy and Threadless, or for activist, for-profit hybrids like Working Assets. Global conglomerates are also sourcing the crowd, not only to build markets but also to take on discomfiting social and environmental challenges. Since 2004, IBM has opened up its technology and business forecasting process to external experts through its Global Innovation

COMPANY-TO-COMPANY COLLABORATION:
NIKE AND CREATIVE COMMONS

On the one hand, Joy's Law, coined by Sun Microsystems cofounder Bill Joy, should cause managers to despair: "No matter who you are, most of the smartest people work for someone else." The Internet, however, has revealed a very bright silver lining to Joy's insight. Although not even a company like Google will loom large enough to claim most of the world's big brains, the Internet has made it possible for any company to connect and collaborate with the nearly 1.6 billion people who now use it.

The trouble is, most companies aren't prepared to solicit the planet's brainpower. They're still organized around a meeting-centric collaboration model, wherein small groups gather online or in person, and the flow of information is tightly controlled. If you aren't in the meeting, you don't know what happened. That narrow corporate mindset hobbles efforts to advance a sustainability agenda; such efforts face challenges far too daunting for any single organization to shoulder alone. As John Wilbanks, the vice president of science at Creative Commons, observes, business "is not harnessing the power of the network to reduce the way we consume resources and achieve sustainability."[20] Creative Commons, a non-profit corporation dedicated to advancing networked collaboration, wants to reverse that sorry state of affairs.

In 2009, Creative Commons, in partnership with Nike and Best Buy, formed an initiative to develop an online, open platform for collaborating on innovations that aim to confront sustainability's challenges. Dubbed the "GreenXchange," the platform operates on a simple but powerful premise: breakthrough sustainability innovations are improved when they're shared. As Natural Path blogger Agnes Mazur asserts, if the GreenXchange "succeeds in changing the way we think about transferring intellectual property and benefiting from shared ideas, it could usher us into a new realm of thinking of sustainability ... as a truly collaborative endeavor."[21]

Though still in its nascent stages at the time of this writing, GreenXchange aims to use Creative Commons' private, voluntary copyright licenses and standardized protocols to make it easier, cheaper, and faster for companies to transfer patents, collaborate on research, and form working groups to attack industry-wide problems. Patent holders determine the terms of use, creating a contract that companies must accept before they dig into the data. Hypersensitive companies can protect their research by shielding it from competitors. All patent holders set the cost of using their intellectual property, which could open up new revenue streams. Even competitive companies, however, should find it useful to collaborate to crack a common threat.

For example, Nike's forecasters project that within the next decade, water scarcity will become a towering environmental challenge for the apparel industry, with spiraling costs to match. The company has embarked on an urgent quest to curb its consumption by developing waterless dyes that can withstand the rigors of sports. By engaging the budding GreenXchange community of academics and businesspeople on that very specific challenge, Nike exponentially increases its innovation potential far beyond the capacity of its internally funded R&D.

Embracing transparency and parceling out hard-won knowledge is scary stuff. Companies have always protected their patents; GreenXchange challenges companies to reveal them. So why did a hypercompetitive innovation machine like Nike, which seems more inclined to crush rivals than to cooperate with them, help launch a platform for sharing intellectual property? And what can the rest of us learn from its lead? Sarah Severn, Nike's director of corporate responsibility horizons, explains.

- *We need to identify what we don't know.* "Nike has a great patent for a 'green rubber' that eliminates five out of the six most toxic chemicals found in the manufacture of rubber-based products," says Severn. "But are there academics out there who could improve on that patent? If there are, GreenXchange might help us find them."

- *Fresh insights often come from the fringe.* "Creative Commons is an uncommon partnership for us, and that's a good thing. They bring in social entrepreneurs and venture capitalists — people who are on the fringes of where we'd normally look for solutions. That's a different community for us to tap into. Hopefully, it will lead us to some different insights."

- *To better compete, cooperate.* "When we collaborate, we get a front-row seat on innovation. We get exposed to far more ideas than any internal R&D team could ever deliver. We've got a lot of smart people at Nike, but we're not half as smart as all the other people out there."

- *We're all in this together.* "All of us in business have been taught to keep what we know in-house, because we want to be the first out the door with a new approach. But business is just not accelerating sustainability efforts at the pace it needs to. In the nearly fifteen years I've been in this role, the world's population has more than doubled. Companies are going to have to get used to sharing resources, both natural and intellectual."

Outlook (GIO) initiative, an ambitious undertaking that recruits some of the world's brightest minds to crack some of the planet's thorniest challenges: health care, economic development in Africa, global climate change, security and society, and more.

IBM is putting its own singular imprint on the innovation-through-collaboration method by sourcing not from the crowd, but from what might best be described as a very elite clique. The GIO consists of invitation-only salons for some of the top thinkers in business, government, and academia. Thus far, IBM has launched more than 75 GIO forums that have brought together more than a thousand experts from dozens of countries, who have forged new relationships, launched working initiatives, and produced an outpouring of ideas.

Case in point: over several months during the fall of 2008, the GIO gathered thought leaders and influencers from such diverse organizations as Coca-Cola Enterprises, Princeton University, and the National Oceanic and Atmospheric Administration. They met in seven international cities—including Atlanta, Amsterdam, Dubai, and Singapore—where they spent the day exploring the one natural resource that's the most critical for every species' survival: water.

Although IBM is a world-beating technology company, its GIO idea-gathering sessions on water and oceans were highly analog. At each "deep dive," as Big Blue calls them, roughly two dozen innovators gathered around a conference table—without their laptops and cell phones—and talked. Their candid, freewheeling conversations dug into strategies for wisely using the planet's vast but finite water supply. The purpose of the GIO forums was not to produce answers but to pose tough questions that might unlock some forward thinking around the future of water and oceans: What are the opportunities that will spur innovation around water management? What are the tradeoffs between water, food, and energy production? What role should the private sector play in ensuring sustainable water supplies?[22]

Though IBM sponsors the salons, they're designed around the open-source model. Any idea that emerges from the conversations is available to anyone who wants to run with it. IBM certainly profits from the sessions, in that it expands its vast ecosystem of partners and it harvests their best thinking to help shape its forecasting and strategic planning. It's no coincidence that a few months after the GIO on water and oceans, IBM rolled out a new line of smart services and technologies to help utilities and companies manage their water supplies more effectively. And it predicted that the market for water services would be worth $20 billion in five years.[23]

But IBM clearly believes that the planet's most precious resource is widely misunderstood and mismanaged. It wants to do something about it, and it wants to help society do something about it. So it published a detailed paper on its water forums and created a GIO group on LinkedIn for participants to continue the conversation. And it's distributed more than a quarter million GIO reports on a variety of topics to businesses, universities, and policymakers around the world.

Big Blue's chairman and chief executive, Sam Palmisano, clearly believes that mutual learning and collaboration is the best way for the company to fulfill a core part of its mission—to ignite innovation that benefits the world. "The work we do together changes the world in meaningful and lasting ways," he wrote in the introduction to *Global Innovation Outlook 2.0.* "My hope is that you'll find here provocative ideas . . . that you can build on and make your own."[24]

How One Small Team Put Hundreds of Heads Together

The challenge for would-be innovators who want to move their companies in a more collaborative direction seems almost insurmountable. How do you make the best case that your company's seasoned strategies for driving innovation could benefit from the radical notion of inviting outsiders to cocreate? How does something as ambitious as the GIO come to be? The answer: it started with a small group of people who thought that even IBM, with all of its intellectual horsepower, would benefit from letting (some of) the outside in.

For anyone who labors in the bland-on-bland environments of most multinationals, it often seems impossible to unleash the kind of dramatic change that open-source collaboration requires. But in 2003, David Yaun and a small group of like-minded peers got the chance. Yaun, in his capacity as vice president of corporate communications at IBM, saw an opportunity to better align Big Blue's profit motive with its values motive. Inspiration came from sourcing the collective wisdom of one of the smartest crowds around—IBM's crowd.

In 2003, as the scandals at Tyco, Worldcom, and Enron made a mockery of those companies' so-called "values," Palmisano redoubled his efforts to ensure that IBM was a purpose-driven organization. For more than eighty years, a shared set of bedrock beliefs—a respect for the individual's dignity and rights, a commitment to excellence, and superior customer service—resided at the core of IBM's culture.[25] But during the early 1990s, as its growth slowed alarmingly and it struggled through the near-death experience of failing to keep pace with its fast-changing industry, Big Blue's priorities shifted from fulfilling its purpose to right-sizing its performance. Knowing, as former IBM president Thomas Watson once wrote, that "the basic philosophy, spirit, and drive of an organization have far more to do with its relative achievements than do technological or economic resources,"[26] Palmisano was determined to restore the primacy of purpose at IBM.

Palmisano realized that the company's values would never be meaningful if they were imposed by corporate fiat. They had to come from an authentic place—from IBMers themselves. He challenged his corporate-communications team to drive a global, company-wide conversation that would identify a set of basic beliefs that would guide IBM in the twenty-first century. They called the initiative the "Values Jam."

Jams had been used before at IBM. In 2001 Big Blue leveraged a massive online brainstorming session to spot emerging business opportunities. The following year it mined ideas for management innovations. But it's doubtful that any company the size of IBM had ever ventured to open-source its values. IBM launched the online equivalent of a town hall meeting and invited its entire global workforce to join in. For three days, thousands of participants tackled questions like "When have you seen IBM at its best?" and "How would the world change if IBM disappeared overnight?" A torrent of responses soon followed. People recalled how IBM's mainframes helped put men on the moon in the 1960s; how the company's IT force got Wall Street running within seventy-two hours after the September 11 terrorist attacks; and how today its advanced-modeling technology detects early-stage breast cancer, saving thousands of lives.

When the Values Jam concluded, IBMers determined that their actions should be driven by three core values, including this one: "Innovation that matters, to the company and *to the world*" (emphasis added). "People weren't interested in innovation for the company's sake only," Yaun told us. "We wanted our innovations to help improve people's lives."[27]

A day after IBM published its newly minted values, more than three thousand employees wrote to Palmisano. Yaun read every email. The messages were overwhelmingly positive. People claimed that the values now spoke to the reasons why they joined the company—to make a difference. The new values statement reawakened a deep sense of pride in the company.

Yet much of the goodwill came with a caveat. More than two-thirds of those who responded hinted that there was a lot of work to be done for IBM to truly live up to its values. Rejecting the PR instinct to hype a feel-good story, Yaun opted to find a way to close the white-space between the rhetoric and the reality of day-to-day life at IBM. He felt compelled to come up with programs that could help change Big Blue's culture, so that all IBMers felt they really could innovate "for the world." But how could a lone PR exec take on such a challenge?

Yaun teamed up with two colleagues, Ed Bevan and Mark Harris, to brainstorm some answers. To them, the key would be *collaborating* with the world. They spent considerable time running down many dead ends. But one day a hallway conversation with IBM's innovation and technology chief, Nick Donofrio, sparked an idea. Donofrio had just come from an annual senior management meeting, dubbed the Global Technology Outlook (GTO), which forecast high-tech developments over the next ten years. Yaun asked him how it went. Donofrio's reply: "We don't know enough about the business and societal implications of what we're seeing."

Yaun shared Donofrio's complaint with Bevan and Harris. What if they were to take the basic construct of the GTO and move it beyond IBM? What if they launched a series of candid conversations about the ways in which technological innovation might generate the greatest benefit for the company and society? But instead of talking amongst themselves, they would include the best and the brightest from other companies, as well as academia, government, and NGOs?

Within an hour, the trio sketched out the basic framework for IBM's Global Innovation Outlook (GIO) program. It would resemble an open-source initiative, whereby challenging global problems are confronted and opportunities for breakthrough innovation are explored. IBM had already committed $1 billion to Linux, which showed Yaun and his colleagues that open-source was redefining innovation and was already becoming a key part of Big Blue's strategy and culture. Linux gave them a model to work from: make the Innovation Outlook effort open, global, multidisciplinary, collaborative—and fun.

In late 2004, five months after Yaun and his team launched the GIO, IBM unveiled the results of the inaugural cycle to three hundred of its top clients. Almost instantly, even the audience began jamming on ideas with onstage participants. Palmisano, who had not planned on speaking, was so stoked by the response that he jumped up and committed IBM's financial and research muscle to the top five ideas to come out of the room.

Now in its fourth generation, the GIO has lately popped up in Second Life, where participants have met "inworld" to explore the future of cities. Moreover, IBM continues to invest millions of dollars in innovations that seek to solve some of the urgent problems explored by the GIO. New, multimillion-dollar businesses in traffic management, electronic health care records, and smart grids, among others, were launched in part by GIO investments.

But the GIO's most significant impact is that it has stitched a core part of IBM's mission—innovation that benefits the world—into the company's cultural fabric. By creating a freewheeling environment for people to grow and share ideas that matter, Yaun's team has established a vivid touchstone for IBMers who might wonder, as they look up from their day-to-day work, whether there's any evidence that Big Blue is living up to its lofty mission.

How did they do it? How did Yaun and his colleagues find a way to surmount a challenge that's as potentially risky and unwieldy as open-sourcing IBM's forecasting process?

They Started from an Authentic Place.

The values that came out of Values Jam are widely regarded as genuine, and the GIO is grafted from Values Jam's rootstock. It's a tangible effort to innovate for the benefit of IBM and for the world. So when Yaun first pitched the GIO concept to IBM associates, many remarked that the idea felt authentic. And because it felt real, a few key executives were more inclined to give it a listen.

They Recruited a Project Champion.

Yaun and his peers had plenty of exposure to IBM's leaders, but comparatively little clout. They knew that their cause required a powerful ally. Once they had blueprinted the design, they pitched it to Donofrio, the company's innovation and technology chief. He immediately saw how the GIO could help IBM identify the intersections at which technological innovation meets emerging business opportunities and social challenges. They demonstrated that the GIO could connect IBM's top researchers with some of the world's top thinkers and influencers. They showed how the resulting relationships and shared learning might accelerate the integration of IBM's technology business with its IT service business. Seeing that it might catalyze one of IBM's core strategies, Donofrio agreed to champion the initiative.

Donofrio wrangled three other high-powered leaders to the GIO cause—the heads of IBM research, consulting, and communications—and arranged an all-important meeting with Palmisano. Their goal: ensure that the GIO wasn't orphaned outside of the company's core business units, like some outlier R&D project. They wanted to drive the GIO through the company and get plenty of buy-in, and they needed the chief's blessing to make that happen. Palmisano readily endorsed the plan and issued a challenge designed to break down internal barriers to change. "Sam told us that if we ever got comfortable doing the project, we were doing it wrong," Yaun recalls. With that, the team had the executive firepower it needed to convert skeptics to the cause.

They Showed How a Do-Good Initiative Is Good for Business.

The GIO is founded on an altruistic impulse: to gather some of the world's biggest brains to crack some of society's most intractable problems. But the project was never presented in altruistic terms. Donofrio and other executives bought into the plan because they believed it made strategic sense. Yaun advocated the notion that providing economic opportunity and achieving, say, sustainable water supplies are naturally aligned goals. The global water crisis represents trillions of dollars of economic activity, it's rife with social and environmental challenges, it spans multiple industries, and it's fertile ground for innovation. In other words, the GIO put IBM right where it wants to be.

GIO's advocates also showed that by tapping the insights of hundreds of outside experts, IBM could widen the lens of its technical and business forecasting processes and increase the likelihood that it would spot the first faintest glimmers of emerging markets. "We want to expand our ecosystem of thought leaders," says Yaun, "and work on the future together."

They Took a Risk But Didn't Gamble.

Yaun and his colleagues thought big, but they didn't necessarily gamble big. After all, they lacked the power to do so. Luckily for them, innovation often involves a fair amount of experimentation, and the GIO's design evolved through trial and error. In the end, they didn't have to risk much to pursue a sizable challenge. They simply had to imagine IBM as a company that really wants to live up to its values, then take a chance on doing something about it.

The GIO team maximized its odds for break-the-mold innovation because they pursued a problem that mattered: to help IBM truly live up to its mission. That inspired others to join in.

Through the GIO, Big Blue provokes a startling range of ideas that it could never equal by itself. The GIO's participants have found that their freewheeling conversations, which bring together varied and sometimes conflicting perspectives from many disciplines, ensure that good ideas get better, especially as the group challenges and critiques them. The GIO itself amounts to a confident admission from one of the world's most admired companies that not even the bright minds inside IBM—an innovation factory that has generated six Nobel laureates and more U.S. patents than any company in the land—are smarter than the many bright minds outside IBM.

Whether it is IBM with its experts, Etsy with its crafters, Threadless with its customers, or Working Assets with its activists, each company understands that the more heads it gets into the mix, the greater the likelihood that it will boost profits and fulfill its larger purpose. These innovators have the humility to admit that they don't have all the answers. They have the deftness to generate the best ideas from the most people. And they have the grit to turn those ideas into game-changing initiatives. They are issuing new challenges to conventional "responsible" companies, which have not yet awoken to the notion that their consumers have more than enough capacity to become valued contributors to their cause.

BEYOND RESPONSIBILITY

7

THE CASE FOR CORPORATE CONSCIOUSNESS

As we discussed in the first chapter, corporate responsibility and, more recently, corporate sustainability have been billed as the way forward for businesses committed to thinking beyond the next quarter and accounting for *all* of their stakeholders, society included. Although this is a critical development, it often falls well short of what is needed.

At too many companies, do-gooding claims are mere marketing pabulum—a way to burnish the brand, entice consumers, and shake off critics. Those companies that are genuinely committed to doing good too often isolate their CR departments from their operating units and so prevent them from influencing critical strategic decisions. Despite the tens of thousands of Web pages and glossy reports declaring that they are stellar corporate citizens, far too many organizations still fail to put sustainability or even responsibility at the very center of their activities.

Something much deeper and more vital is required—something that those who are inventing the future of corporate responsibility call "corporate consciousness." The two words don't often go together. Absolutists like Robert Reich, a political commentator and professor at Berkeley who served as secretary of labor under Bill Clinton, argue that a corporation is a legal entity whose sole responsibility is to its officers, employees, and shareholders—but not to society.[1] In Reich's view, "Corporations are pieces of paper. They are contractual agreements."[2] There is no "corporate responsibility"—at least not in the way that most of us have come to understand the term. Corporations aren't moral; they aren't immoral. Nor are they conscious or conscientious.

We disagree. Even in a legal sense, corporations hold many of the responsibilities normally accorded to individuals. They sue and are sued. They are held accountable for breaking the law and for paying their debts. They buy and sell property. A corporation is "born" when its members obtain a certificate of incorporation, and it "dies" when it bleeds money and becomes insolvent.[3]

In her insightful book *The Divine Right of Capital,* Marjorie Kelly observes that businesses frequently claim the same rights as individuals, which ironically has helped them abuse their power, as when they argue that corporate campaign contributions are the same as free speech and are therefore protected. The long-term value of a business rests not in its certificate of incorporation nor even in its bank account or physical assets, but in the talent and knowledge of its associates. Kelly uses the real-life example of an ad agency whose employees left en masse and took their accounts with them. Once they'd gone, the company was essentially worthless.[4]

The term "corporate" emanates from the Latin *corporatus* or "made into a body," and anyone who visits a business can't help but see it for what it truly is: a voluntary "body" of individuals engaged in a common pursuit. If the corporation is to succeed—if it is to grow revenue and contribute positively to society—it must have a high degree of unified consciousness. That is, individual members must be acutely aware of their effect on other group members as well as on the world around them. They should be ever mindful of the values that define the group's collective purpose and the imperatives that guide its progress. The word itself implies a collaborative endeavor: "conscious" is derived from the Latin *conscius*, "having common knowledge with another."

The problem is, most companies never do the hard work of developing that "common knowledge," at either the individual or the organizational level. They fail to intentionally and collectively forge a coherent view of what the enterprise's ambition should be. Without a clearly articulated view of what matters most to the company and the willingness to apply it in day-to-day decision making, associates often work at cross-purposes, leaders lose their way, the company unleashes a host of unintended impacts on society and the environment, and its declarations of "corporate responsibility" inevitably ring hollow.

Since 2005, Seventh Generation, in collaboration with the author and consultant Carol Sanford, has sought to define and grow its collective consciousness.[5] Sanford has helped both Fortune 500 companies and start-ups exercise a way of thinking that brings both flexibility and discipline to their strategic planning and execution. For Seventh Generation, developing a higher level of awareness of the way we work and what we want to accomplish gives us a better shot at fulfilling the lofty goals we have set for ourselves.

Seventh Generation's effort to grow its consciousness parallels the argument put forth in the remarkable book *Presence: An Exploration of Profound Change in People, Organizations, and Society*.[6] The book underlines the notion that much of the way we move through life falls within deeply grooved patterns of habit. The way we start our workday, read the newspaper, conduct ourselves in a meeting, watch a sunset—most of what we do, we do as we've done before. The result is that more often than not, the possibility of achieving real change resides outside of our self-imposed mental models. Whether it's designing a better product, spying a breakthrough business opportunity, becoming a better parent—those unrealized achievements are to be found in behavioral territory we rarely (if ever) visit. *Presence* persuasively argues that if we reflect on how we think and if we question whether there's a better way, a whole new world of possibility opens up to us.

Awakening our individual consciousness and yoking it to a collective sense of purpose is inherently a *"de-stabilizing* process," as Carol Sanford describes it. It requires that we move from being a "functionally static" organization that operates largely by rote to a "functionally dynamic" organization that continually challenges and improves the way we do things. It means we must break our ingrained habits of thinking, kick over stale ideas, reexamine our emotional patterns and language archetypes, and avoid the easy path of simply repeating past successes. Only then can we raise the bar on what is possible.

Has Seventh Generation succeeded? There's really no end to the journey—it's more of an endless process of becoming increasingly self-aware. It's been a challenging effort that has tested the spirit and will of each and every associate. Old patterns of thinking about the role of business in society sometimes limits people from accomplishing more; fear of change sometimes leads others to settle for less. But so far, the business results speak for themselves. Despite confronting a mob of upstart challengers and a full-on assault from Godzilla itself (aka Clorox), Seventh Generation's sales of sustainable household and personal-care products grew by 45 percent in 2007 and 51 percent in a tumultuous 2008, when the depth of the economic downturn caught even seasoned analysts off guard. In 2009, as the economy slid further into the abyss of a deep recession, the company still managed to achieve modest (albeit much slower) growth and continued to poach A+ talent from some of its biggest competitors.

Just as important, Seventh Generation boosted its "return on purpose." The effort to become a conscious corporate citizen led us to roll out a slew of initiatives that aim to lessen our environmental impact, nourish society, and inspire other enterprises to do the same. This collective self-awareness fuels associates' inner drive to create change and reflects a deeper sense of knowing not only our strengths but also, and more important, our weaknesses and the pitfalls that await us as we move into a challenging future. Seventh Generation has learned first-hand that developing and harnessing human consciousness, as Carol Sanford argues, is both a "fundamental executive task ... and the underlying principle for growing businesses."[7]

TO BUILD CORPORATE CONSCIOUSNESS: SEVENTH GENERATION

"Corporate consciousness" may exude a whiff of the mystical (or at least, the mysterious), but at its core, it's really about clarity of purpose. It points the way for people to contribute meaningfully to a shared vision of what matters most to the organization, and ensures they develop a clear picture of what success looks like. In Seventh Generation's case, building a corporate consciousness means striving to ensure that "sustainability" does not belong in some outlier department, but in the heart and mind of every associate, to ensure that we first conceive, and then seek to create, a promising future.

At too many companies, too few people are responsible for responsibility. At Seventh Generation, corporate consciousness engages the entire community in the work that's most important. When it clicks, it commits the company to the notion that furthering sustainability—a task that includes social justice and equity—is everyone's job, from accounting to marketing, logistics to product development. And it reminds people that in all of their work, they should strive to live up to the name the company derived from the Great Law of the Iroquois Confederacy: "In our every deliberation, we must consider the impact of our decisions on the next seven generations."

Our company's name, and the deep heritage from which it arises, implies that we seek to bring a higher level of consciousness to all of our work. "In *our* every deliberation" signals that we think and act collectively in all that we do. Before we decide, we discuss. (Some will say we discuss too much and too often.) Our ideas aren't formed in isolation; our consumers and stakeholders inform them.

The next part of the quotation, "we must consider the *impact* of our decisions," compels us to think systemically and understand our place in the larger whole. That is, we must recognize that all of our actions, the bad as well as the good, ripple out from the company and affect consumers and competitors, as well as the community, society, and the environment.

The final part of the quote, "on the next *seven generations*," suggests that we're not simply working for the here and now. Far from it. Our real "corporate responsibility" as the op-ed columnist David Brooks asserts, is to the generations of "unborn people we will never meet." Brooks calls such forward thinking the "power of posterity." It's an obligation to create a better future, which infuses our work with meaning and "give[s] us the gift of our way of life."[8]

Taken together, the words of the Great Law eloquently express the idea that the future of society and the environment are temporarily entrusted to our care. The Law gave Seventh Generation its animating spirit and set us on the road to bringing a higher level of consciousness to our work.

To define and grow a collective consciousness is to develop a clear line of sight into a company's essence, or *true identity*—the values and characteristics that make up the company's fundamental beliefs; its *global imperatives*—long-term pursuits that benefit society and the planet; and its *corporate direction*—the lens that brings business and social purpose into sharp focus and enhances the organization's performance. Let's unpack these terms and show how they attempt to ensure that Seventh Generation's business strategy flows directly out of its commitment to move far beyond conventional definitions of corporate responsibility.

Rediscovering the Organization's True Identity

Every venture, at its inception, is instilled with a core purpose and set of beliefs. These emanate from the company's founders and its very first hires—the core group that forms the company's DNA and sets it on its cultural path. Amazon's workplace culture, for example, is "obsessed with today's customer" in large part because its founder, Jeff Bezos, is extraordinarily customer-focused. In an interview with the *Harvard Business Review*, Bezos's phrasing is inelegant but his sense of purpose is clear: "Years from now, when people look back at Amazon, I want them to say that we uplifted customer-centricity across the entire business world."[9] It's unthinkable that some corporate do-gooding committee could impose a different mission on Amazon; such a quest must spring organically from the founder's vision and the company's "soul."

Companies that are authentically purpose driven are keenly aware of the beliefs, values, and characteristics that make them unique. Google's mission to "organize the world's information" feels real because it continues to reflect its cofounders' milieu—Silicon Valley and Stanford University's School of Engineering—where innovation, entrepreneurship, and the pursuit of knowledge are highly valued. It is often remarked that even though he died in 1992, Sam Walton's "presence" continues to loom large in Wal-Mart's Bentonville headquarters. In fact, veteran executives, when faced with a difficult decision, still sometimes ask, "WWSD"—what would Sam do?[10] Despite its many flaws, Wal-Mart has stayed true to its core value, "always low prices," because it hasn't strayed far from its core identity—the frugality, focus, and work ethic that flow from its founder.

Although the genetic code of a company's culture is imprinted during its earliest days, its beliefs and values often recede into the background as people focus on the urgent task of growing the business. If the enterprise survives and prospers, there inevitably comes a time when significant success forces people to confront a conundrum: What's our purpose? Where are we headed? What should our business accomplish over the next three, five, or even ten years?

That's where Seventh Generation found itself in 2005. After seventeen years, the company was making money and growing rapidly—sales had jumped 37 percent over the previous year. It had enjoyed a wave of recognition for its corporate responsibility work—acclaim that cemented its leadership position in the field.[11] Despite such progress, Seventh Generation was unwittingly operating on the time-tested principle that says if you don't know where you are going, any road will take you there.

Although Seventh Generation's purpose may have seemed obvious to outsiders, from the inside it wasn't at all clear. In an effort to be inclusive and embrace the entire team's sundry ideas, the company had increasingly begun to pursue many different directions at once, some of which were in direct conflict with others: growth, profitability, education, advocacy, developing consumer products, becoming a model of corporate responsibility, creating a great place to work, saving the planet, making the world a better place. People were juggling a dozen different agendas; collisions and slip-ups were the inevitable result. That's when the company brought Carol Sanford into its fold and began the work to uncover its core identity and use it to help frame the enterprise's strategic direction.

Rediscovering an organization's essence is akin to an archeological expedition: you dig deep into the company's past to uncover the beliefs and values established during the enterprise's earliest days. For Seventh Generation, this inward-looking journey began with a three-step exercise that defined how staffers view, or *process,* the world; identified what they *value;* and clarified what they believe is the enterprise's fundamental *purpose.* In many respects, Seventh Generation's essence reflects its cofounder's core identity. So to better reveal the company's heart and soul, Jeffrey started with his own inner exploration.

Core Process

Jeffrey defined his core process—how he perceives and works in the world—as "reconciling systemic dissonance," a fancy way of saying that he is driven to confront the big things in life that don't add up. For example, we compete in a system in which companies maximize profits by offloading the indirect costs of, say, their contribution to air or groundwater pollution. The result is that society pays the price. So organic produce is more expensive than conventionally grown food, but only because we fail to charge Big Agriculture for the full cost of its calamitous effects on workers' health and the environment. Equally problematic, only wealthier consumers can afford the healthiest and safest products. Such "systemic dissonance" has a direct, negative impact on the business, as Seventh Generation fails to sell the bulk of its natural and nontoxic products at a price point that's affordable for the lower-income folks who need them most.

In today's world, there's no shortage of systems that are out of whack. We grow enough food to feed much of the world, yet many go hungry. We have the knowledge and capability to power the world with renewable energy, yet we continue to burn fossil fuels. For Seventh Generation, the challenge lies in deciding which big, pervasive problems to overcome—and in decoding their underlying causes before taking corrective action.

Core Value

It was easier to surface Jeffrey's core value, which is also one of this book's core principles: to live authentically. Seventh Generation has spent more than two decades practicing "authenticity," even though we know it's highly unlikely we'll ever fully achieve it. We've learned it's the often painful process of revealing our failures and mistakes, rather than heralding our successes, that edge us closer to the real ideal.

In 2003, in Seventh Generation's first corporate responsibility report, Jeffrey acknowledged, "many of our products are not as authentic to our environmental mission as we would like them to be." To deepen consumers' understanding of the tough trade-offs between pursuing sustainability and improving performance, the company used the report to critique some of its own wares—a practice that continues to this day. It's good to be right, but sometimes we are most authentically ourselves when we concede we are wrong.

Core Purpose

A company's core purpose is not the same as its core value proposition, but it nevertheless creates great value. Jeff Bezos understood this when he claimed that Amazon does more than provide the best information about the product it sells (its value proposition)—it also helps consumers make better buying decisions (its purpose).

Jeffrey's core purpose is to strive to make the world a little more equitable, a little less unjust—goals that aren't exactly high on most alpha capitalists' agendas. Achieving universal access to high-quality health care and education, setting a minimum wage that's actually livable, ensuring that women are paid the same as men for comparable work—all too often, justice and equity fall beyond the bounds of business's hypercompetitive, winner-take-all playing field. Although Seventh Generation hasn't succeeded often enough in advancing these causes, it's essential that the company continue to try to expand its positive impact. It makes little sense to launch efforts that seek to restore the environment to full health and not attempt to do the same for society. In a world where other businesses are discovering sustainable products, Seventh Generation aspires to be a sustainable company.

One real-world initiative that sprang from defining the company's core purpose is Seventh Generation's collaboration with Oakland, California–based WAGES (Women's Action to Gain Economic Security), a non-profit that creates jobs and empowers low-income Latinas by organizing and incubating cooperative businesses.

Seventh Generation is committed to helping WAGES create cooperative house-cleaning businesses throughout the United States. The venture requires investments of capital and business know-how, in the same way that economic returns require them. WAGES provides the initial organizing, training, business systems, support, and nurturing that the cooperatives need in order to become self-sustaining enterprises. But WAGES can't expand these efforts without our assistance. That's why Seventh Generation has paid the salaries of WAGES managers, assisted in training cooperative members on health and safety issues, and used the company's brand to help promote the co-ops' services.

Admittedly, WAGES and Seventh Generation's half-dozen other social initiatives only begin to push the company toward becoming an enterprise that truly fulfills its core purpose—to create a just and equitable society. But they are a big part of what animates the organization. The sense of advocacy that defines Seventh Generation in the marketplace is driven by a palpable sense of purpose in the workplace, and that purpose flows directly out of the company's essence.

Core Process, Value, and Purpose = Corporate Essence

Reveal systemic dissonance. Live authentically. Create a just and equitable world. In the seventeen years prior to their work with Carol Sanford, Seventh Generation's associates had made that triad their own. But they had done so almost unconsciously. New hires would often remark that they were drawn to Seventh Generation because of its values, but they couldn't really articulate them. And neither could we. Although the work to develop a collective consciousness began with Jeffrey—and was led internally by Gregor Barnum, our "director of corporate consciousness"—the intent was never to impose the cofounder's vision on the rest of the organization. Rather, it was to unearth a true company identity that had never been clearly enough defined to sharpen our strategic focus.

MEETINGS WITH A PURPOSE

As part of our effort to bring a higher degree of alertness or consciousness to our work, Seventh Generation engages in a series of everyday practices that help associates think together in a more aligned way. One of these work rituals is a variation of a "Task Cycle," a concept we learned from consultant Carol Sanford.[12] It's a brief statement of purpose that helps ensure that we never launch a group effort without first asking what we're doing, why we're doing it, and what we intend to accomplish.

Prior to organizing a meeting or project, the team leader draws up a task cycle and shares it with the group. The statement gives people a framework for thinking in advance about the initiative's purpose, the results or "products" they want to create, the effect they hope to have, and the process they'll use to execute the work.

Each task cycle hews to the exact same format and employs consistent language (which is italicized in the quotations that follow). In 2009, the purpose statement written for the task cycle that helped organize Seventh Generation's companywide, strategy-update meeting led with this objective: *"To create understanding of* the strategy work, which provides the foundation for 2009 and future planning." This alerts people to the notion that we don't just want to pursue some open-ended objective; we want to provoke a change or transformation, such as a clearer line of sight into our competitive landscape.

The statement next described the benefit to the greater good: *"In a way that* enables the Seventh Generation community to understand decisions . . . and their impacts." It concluded by defining the desired outcome: *"So that* every member of the community can connect their work to Seventh Generation's business strategy." The intent is to push beyond a narrow, internal view of tasks and goals, and instead produce a systems view of our work and all of its impacts.

In a sense, a task cycle functions as a kind of "premortem": it pushes us to collectively anticipate a project's pitfalls and opportunities *before* they unfold. It shows people at the start of the meeting what we hope to accomplish by the end of the meeting. That kind of clarity and direction setting raises the level of engagement, and it signals that no one can be a bystander. Equally important, we ensure that we stay on track during the meeting by pausing to reflect on what's been said. By thinking in advance—and taking timeouts to ensure that we're actively thinking together—we usually make the meeting much more effective. And, we're happy to report, much shorter.

Once those beliefs and values were brought back into the bright light of day, people worked hard to articulate them. Values are worthless if they don't factor into day-to-day thinking. So at every big company meeting, associates didn't simply show a slide that defined the three core elements of the company's identity. They also took turns making it palpable by drawing it up on flip charts and white boards, telling stories and bringing it to bear in conversations. Such efforts sought to ensure that people's decisions were aligned with the company's values.

Having reawakened the company's true sense of itself, people began to have a clearer understanding of what they were working for. But that insight did not come easily, and we had to constantly strive to hold on to it. That meant continually questioning our assumptions, speaking up when our actions failed to align with our values, and provoking each other to think differently. So long as we felt a little off balance—a little destabilized—we knew we were scrambling up the right path.

Developing the Company's Global Imperatives

The effort to unearth the company's true corporate essence was very much an inward-looking journey; in contrast, developing our global imperatives was not unlike an untethered space walk into the future. Global imperatives are long-term pursuits that guide Seventh Generation's efforts to grow the business and contribute to society. They could take a century or more to achieve. By that yardstick, they are not unlike

Google's open-ended ambition to "organize the world's information" or Genzyme's quest to "innovate on behalf of people with serious diseases." But as the language suggests, global imperatives are not the same as a mission.

A mission defines the task or objective that the enterprise hopes to accomplish, however broad and bold.[13] An imperative is a call to action. A mission grows out of the question, "What should we do for the world?" An imperative poses the question that arose in the first chapter, "What does the world need most that we can best provide?" That question lies at the heart of Seventh Generation's beliefs about the purpose and possibility of business; it serves as a reminder that we intend to be a different kind of company. It also compels associates to reflect deeply on the world's needs and the company's capabilities; it pushes them to explore how they can best respond to the considerable challenges (and boundless opportunities) that confront us all. Pursuing imperatives requires a complicated mix of many efforts: cooperating with other businesses and organizations and furthering our own ongoing education and development.

"What does the world most need from us?" Associates put the question on a whiteboard and began to answer it in autumn 2005, at the annual all-company retreat in Stowe, Vermont. To make the global imperatives feel authentic, the entire Seventh Generation community weighed in on them. To give the process sufficient focus, an advance team spent the earlier part of the year creating a working draft of the GIs, as we came to call them. The eight imperatives that grew out of that company-wide meeting were scary and inspiring, hopeful and imposing.

The original language, however, was overly opaque, which made the imperatives hard to remember and even harder to use. In 2007, the GIs were pared down to 236 words—still too long and too knotty. In 2009, we tried again, smoothing the kinks and cutting the document by nearly two-thirds. When we presented the draft in a May staff meeting, some associates pushed back hard. They argued that in simplifying the language we had diluted the heart of the message. So we went back and included some concepts that, although somewhat abstract, still held a powerful part of our purpose. For example, one imperative that was sorely missed when we presented the abbreviated version—so we subsequently added it back in—is "Holding the past, the present, and the future in the same mind, we will create a world rich in values as contrasted to a world rich in artifacts."

No doubt, our global imperatives will continue to evolve. But throughout the editing effort, the core imperatives have persisted. They require that Seventh Generation work to restore the environment, help create a world that is "just and equitable," and encourage associates to think of themselves as educators dedicated to inspiring "conscious consumption."[14]

If those goals sound impossibly utopian, that is partly the intent. Global imperatives compel us to imagine the world at its very best and then act as a force for positive change. Taken together, they are arguably unattainable—at least in the near term. And truth be told, they still aren't always memorable. We're still struggling to make them cohere. What matters is that, by and large, most associates intuit the GIs' aim, even if they can't always articulate it.

The global imperatives' real benefit is that they begin to answer the question, what makes Seventh Generation different? They give associates permission to reimagine what it means to compete in the consumer packaged goods (CPG) industry. Indeed, in a fundamental sense, Seventh Generation isn't even in the CPG business. As our ultimate imperative asserts, we're in the business of "inspiring conscious consumption." We are committed to teaching ourselves, our business partners, consumers, and even our competitors to consider how their decisions today impact future generations.

Although that sounds a little starry-eyed, it doesn't mean people sway to the rhythms of "We Are the World." Defining ourselves as evangelists for conscious consumption sets the company apart and amounts to a key competitive weapon in an industry that's dominated by "stack 'em high and price 'em low" thinking. Seventh Generation has flourished as a business because associates view themselves as knowledge resources and coaches, not simply as purveyors of diapers and dish liquids. For them, "educate" means "activate."

For example, in 2008, Seventh Generation launched the "Show the World What's Inside" campaign, which focused on educating and promoting full ingredient disclosure in household cleaning products. Federal regulations require food companies to display on their packaging a complete list of the ingredients in their cookies and processed soups, and personal-care companies to declare the chemicals in their shampoos. Unfortunately, the brands that market laundry, dishwashing, and other cleaners aren't required to reveal what's in the bottle, even though some of the chemicals found in conventional cleaners are known or probable carcinogens.[15]

Seventh Generation had already begun to voluntarily disclose the ingredients in all of its cleaning products by listing them on its labels and on the Material Safety Data Sheets posted on its Web site. Some companies followed our lead. But the majority didn't.

So Seventh Generation educated and agitated for widespread change throughout the industry by launching Show What's Inside. This multifaceted effort included an educational Web site and an online Label Reading Guide, downloadable to shoppers' cell phones, which helped them interpret labels at the point of purchase and understand the potential risks in many household-cleaning products. The company also supported the Environmental Working Group's campaign to help consumers become activists by prompting them to call on regulators for greater ingredient transparency and to support the "Kid-Safe Chemical Act." When the makers of household cleaning products are pressed to reveal the dangerous chemicals in some of their ingredients, presumably they'll change their products' formulas to make them safer.

Not long after Seventh Generation launched Show What's Inside, SC Johnson cloned its version of an ingredient-disclosure effort. The maker of Windex, Glade, Raid, and other billion-dollar brands followed our lead by creating a campaign dubbed "What's Inside." That was just what we had hoped for. When a $7.5 billion giant like SC Johnson puts its brawn behind ingredient disclosure, it's likely that the rest of the industry will follow, regardless of what regulators do.

The unique sense of purpose that associates derive from Seventh Generation's global imperatives drives the company's strategy, from the initiatives it promotes and the markets it enters right down to the products it develops and the people it hires. The GIs not only push people to raise the bar on sustainability, but also affirm the notion that as long as we imagine a brighter future, we can make a bigger difference. The GIs catalyze the larger goal of prodding business to embrace a whole new mind-set—one that moves from thinking incrementally about doing less harm to thinking expansively about leaving things better than we found them.

Setting the Corporate Direction

Having defined who we are (the company's essence) and what we intend to do (global imperatives), the third challenge was to map out where we're headed—that is, the domain in which the company will do its work. Seventh Generation's corporate direction is designed to define the company's work as it seeks to fulfill its imperatives. Setting a corporate direction is very much a focusing process—something we're not very good at. It's as much about deciding what we *won't* do as what we will do.

Corporate direction allows you to get big and stay focused. Just consider W. L. Gore & Associates. Best known for its GORE-TEX laminate, this Delaware-based innovation machine produces a range of products so vast that it's difficult to take it all in: fabrics for gloves, running shoes, and sleeping bags; synthetic vascular grafts and surgical meshes; coaxial cables, premium guitar strings, even dental floss. But Gore doesn't pursue just any opportunity to develop a new product. It's interested only in innovations that grow out of polytetrafluoroethylene (PTFE), the slick fluoropolymer better known by its brand name, Teflon. In a sense, Gore's corporate direction—all the things it will do and the only things it will do—is defined by PTFE.

In Seventh Generation's case, setting our corporate direction was an extraordinarily challenging process. After seventeen years of teasing out who we were and what we believed in, it was tough to bring discipline and focus to our mission and vision. In the sensitive and inclusive culture we had created, we found it difficult to articulate what we *weren't* going to be. But after more than a few heated debates, we set a direction that defines our strategic goal—"to lead the field of sustainability and corporate responsibility"—and identifies where and how we will pursue it—"at the intersection of human and environmental health, through personal care and home care systems."

Corporate direction is the glue that binds the enterprise to the specific expression of its true identity and its global imperatives, while providing strategic focus. It allows everyone in the company to think in an aligned way. No matter how inviting, if an opportunity doesn't positively contribute to human health and the environment, or if it's unrelated to home care or personal care, we'll try to pass it up—though in many cases that's easier said than done.

Most companies' declarations of responsibility and sustainability are greeted with skepticism, because consumers perceive that companies rarely use those values to frame their business objectives, let alone work to ensure that they're alive and well in associates' hearts and minds. At Seventh Generation, we bring our global imperatives and corporate direction to bear on many major decisions, not only because it's the authentic thing to do, but also because it's the *strategic* thing to do. It helps us define, over the next three to five years, what sustainability will look like in the home care and personal care business. And it lets us build a strategy that keeps us in the forefront. Developing our corporate consciousness is as competitive as anything we do.

CORPORATE CONSCIOUSNESS FRAMES CORPORATE STRATEGY

Corporate consciousness is a counterweight to the copycat thinking that permeates so much of business in general and the consumer packaged goods industry in particular. It often seems that many big CPG companies are content to be masters of incremental (and often meaningless) change. So much of their "innovation" is really about launching new colors ("whiter than white!") and concocting new scents ("fresher than a mountain stream!")—trifling benefits that most of us could easily do without. Seventh Generation competes in an industry that is forever trying to make life better at the margins, without ever delving into those things that produce sustainable, lasting value. For many companies, strategy is nothing more than finding the most willing buyer, in the biggest category, with the best price point. Their strategic discussions obviously start with the same questions, because they invariably reach the same conclusions: improve the product, drop the cost, sharpen the marketing campaign. After that, it's simply a race for second place.

Seventh Generation aims to arrive at a different place. We seek to avoid thinking first about margins or markets. That should come much later in our discussions. At the outset, we try to preface big strategic decisions with two unconventional questions: does the opportunity align with our global imperatives? Will it set a higher standard and provide real value? If we can prove that it does, we know that it comes from an authentic place and builds on our animating purpose. We then ask, if we pursue the opportunity, do we have the "ableness"—the skill, will, and resources—to win? That is, will the opportunity lead to an innovation that will significantly disrupt our industry?

Admittedly, this is not the conventional way to set strategy. Garry Embleton, who put in executive stints at P&G and Clorox before becoming our chief of strategic sourcing, says he's never seen anything quite like it. "How many CPG companies, when they think about getting into a new business, start with their mission and corporate direction statements? I genuinely believe it never happens."

Because we use our own unique values and mission to set strategy, we have a better shot at creating an original blueprint for the future of our business and our industry—not just in terms of economics but also in terms of expectations. We put ourselves in a better position to raise the bar on what's possible for our associates, stakeholders, competitors, and consumers. That's what we hoped to accomplish in 2009, when we set out to become the first CPG company in North America to tackle the challenge of palm-oil production and its destructive effect on tropical rainforests and the local communities, by using sustainably grown palm oil in our cleaning products.

Most people would think that a product made from palm oil is more natural and sustainable than one made from petroleum. We did, and we were wrong. Palm oil is the world's top-selling vegetable oil; as much as 50 percent of the products on supermarket shelves contain it.[16] But its success has come at a profound social and ecological cost.

Over the past couple of decades, there's been a nearly sixfold increase in palm-oil production. To make way for large-scale plantations, vast tracts of old-growth rainforest in places like Indonesia and Malaysia have been clear-cut. Such deforestation releases vast quantities of CO_2, significantly adding to global climate change,[17] and it deprives some of the world's most endangered species of their key habitats. Palm-oil production drives indigenous people from their land and spews pesticides into the air and groundwater. In using traditional palm oil in most of our cleaning products, we were failing to live up to two of our core imperatives: to help make the world more "just and equitable" and to "restore our environment."

In our effort to trace the path "from the soil to the bottle" and thereby attain a deeper understanding of the ecological and social dimensions of our ingredients, Seventh Generation zeroed in on palm oil—our cleaner lines' largest component. If palm oil isn't produced sustainably, then neither are our cleaners. Two of our sourcing experts flew to Riau Province in Sumatra, the front line for palm-oil industry development in Indonesia. Their first-hand account of the rapid conversion of tropical rainforest to palm-oil plantations, along with our global imperatives, virtually required that we attempt to develop a market for sustainable palm oil.

Though we're still in the early stages of the journey, we've made some noteworthy headway. Seventh Generation became the first company in our industry to purchase sustainable palm oil "production credits," modeled on carbon credits, to cover the company's palm-oil consumption across our entire cleaning product portfolio. By paying a premium to producers of sustainable palm, Seventh Generation supports their work and begins to expand the market for greener palm-oil production. Purchasing oil credits is just the first step in a broader strategy that will culminate in sourcing a dedicated supply of sustainable palm oil for use in our products.

Seventh Generation's pursuit of sustainable palm oil synchronizes seamlessly with our corporate direction, which requires us to lead "at the intersection of human and environmental health." It differentiates the company and thereby puts us in a position to disrupt our industry. Although conventional CPG companies vie for competitive advantage on the margins (slightly better products, slightly lower cost), we have the opportunity to build an entirely new market category.

Equally important, our efforts to support and expand the sustainable palm-oil industry fulfill the imperative that we educate—or, more to the point, that we influence. We intend to be first, but we also intend that our competitors follow. So we're working to take some of the risk and complexity out of building a supply chain for sustainable palm, knowing that it will clear the way for many in our industry to join the cause. In that way, we scale our impact. As we do so, we'll lose our point of differentiation. But no matter. Seventh Generation will set a higher standard and continue to raise the bar.

Part of the purpose behind Seventh Generation's effort to develop a corporate consciousness is to push our partners and competitors to adopt our definition of success as their standard operating procedure. If they emulate what we do, we just might help lead business to a better place. We know it won't be easy. Our clear-eyed take on our own performance shows that many of us at Seventh Generation still struggle to break old patterns of thinking, still question whether it's smart to build strategy around a cause, and still fear what change might bring. Yet we remain convinced that the only way that business can stand for something special is to put mission and meaning before margins and markets. When we bring a higher level of consciousness to our work, good things tend to follow.

ACTION ITEM: FIRST STEPS FOR DEVELOPING CORPORATE CONSCIOUSNESS AT YOUR COMPANY

1. Ask a large swath of your company's associates (or, if possible, the whole community): what does the world most need that we can uniquely provide?
2. Unearth the company's essence, or core identity, by identifying its purpose, work process, and values.

3. Conduct cross-departmental meetings to openly and honestly confront two questions:
   - Where are our actions out of alignment with our values?
   - What can we do to ensure greater alignment?
4. Follow-up meetings should focus on two additional challenges:
   - What principles should guide how we work together?
   - What are we unwilling to be transparent about, and why?
5. Answers to the above questions will help frame the thinking for this final question: what's our specific business case for forging a more responsible and sustainable company?

EPILOGUE

Throughout this book, we've sought to show that when companies shift their value proposition from selling desirable products to solving difficult social and environmental problems, whole new opportunities arise; that when they reframe their conventional notions about what it means to act responsibly, they move from thinking incrementally about doing less harm to thinking expansively about leaving things better than they found them.

At every opportunity, we've argued that companies must push past conventional definitions of corporate responsibility. And many will, as they bend to the demands of consumers and employees and realize that the future promises scarcer resources and accelerating expectations that business should contribute to the greater good. By digging into a disparate swath of revolutionary good companies, we've sought to demonstrate that the best way to raise the bar on responsibility is to innovate around those six core principles: mission and collaboration, transparency and authenticity, community and consciousness.

We've seen how companies as varied as Novo Nordisk and Linden Lab, Nike and Etsy, Seventh Generation and IBM have leveraged these principles to achieve new performance thresholds. We've watched how company leaders, as well as those a few steps down the organizational ladder, have demonstrated that corporate responsibility is now about innovation, not simply reputation.

The question is, who's next? Who's going to surpass the conventional, incremental approach to furthering sustainability? Who's going to show that when companies aspire to more, they often achieve more? Our hope is that it's you. Admittedly, it's an unnerving challenge. But all it takes is a first step. And as we've seen at eBay, Patagonia, IBM, and elsewhere, just about anyone at any level of an organization can take it. Our final suggestion: as you embark on this journey, you might hold in mind a question and a quotation.

At the book's outset, we posed a question that pushes companies to define their core purpose: "What does the world most need that we are uniquely able to provide?" Now it's your turn. Change the "we" in that question to an "I." Our ability to transform the world into a more sustainable, more equitable place starts with our own definition of the role we're willing to play. All possibility begins in our own hearts and minds.

In the final chapter, we cited the quotation from which Seventh Generation derives its name: "In our every deliberation, we must consider the impact of our decisions on the next seven generations." As we noted, the quote comes from the founding document of the Iroquois Confederacy. Created in the late sixteenth century, the Great Law brought together five northern Iroquois tribes that were previously in a state of constant, internecine warfare. The Law revitalized the tribes by organizing them into matriarchal clans and emphasizing equality, consent of the governed, and, above all, the notion that what we do today defines tomorrow. The Law still resonates powerfully, and we believe it embodies the philosophy we must all embrace to make the world a better place.

Over the years, people have suggested that Seventh Generation change its name to something that's "clearer" and "contemporary" (whatever that means). We have resisted. Our name, although challenging, has a beautiful, rich heritage. We'll spend the rest of our lives trying to live up to it. We humbly invite you to do the same.

The hard-won lessons we've learned first-hand at Seventh Generation, as well as through the revolutionaries whom we've met in this book, show that business *can,* in fact, help build a better world than the one we've inherited. The goal of replenishing society and the environment is certainly within our grasp, so long as we cut through the constraints of settling for what's acceptable and dare to imagine what's transformational. The next generations demand nothing less.

NOTES

PREFACE

1 Peter M. Senge, Bryan Smith, Sara Schley, Joe Laur, and Nina Kruschwitz, *The Necessary Revolution: How Individuals and Organizations Are Working Together to Create a Sustainable World* (New York: Doubleday, 2008).

CHAPTER ONE

1 "Triodos" is derived from the Greek *tri hodos,* or "threefold way," which describes the logic behind its investing strategy: social, environmental, and financial.

2 Quoted from an interview with the authors.

3 Some prefer "corporate social responsibility," or CSR, to "corporate responsibility."

4 Gould developed the theory with the paleontologist Niles Eldredge.

5 Adam Smith, *The Theory of Moral Sentiments* (Cambridge University Press, 2002), p. 1.

6 Drucker is quoted by David Cooperrider, director of Case Western Reserve University's Center for Business as Agents of World Change, in "The Business Case for Social Responsibility," ASAE & the Center for Association Leadership; http://www.asaecenter.org/PublicationsResources/content.cfm?ItemNumber=27918.

7 Lee Scott resigned as CEO of Wal-Mart in February 2009.

8 Jeremy Oppenheim, Sheila Bonini, Debby Bielak, Tarrah Kehm, and Peter Lacy, "Shaping the New Rules of Competition: UN Global Compact Participant Mirror," McKinsey & Company, July 2007.

9 Daniel Franklin, "Just Good Business," *The Economist*, January 17, 2008.

10 M. Todd Henderson and Anup Malani, "Capitalism 2.0," *Forbes*, March 10, 2008.

11 Speech by Patrick Cescau, group chief executive of Unilever, at the 2007 INDEVOR Alumni Forum in INSEAD, Fontainebleau, France (May 25, 2007).

12 Quoted by Jo Marchant, "Interview: The Environmental Activist," *New Scientist*, October 15, 2008.

13 Bryan Walsh, "Gambling on Green," *Time*, December 12, 2007.

14 Quoted from Google's "Company Overview," http://www.google.com/corporate/.

15 As described by Whole Foods cofounder and CEO John Mackey in his article, "Rethinking the Social Responsibility of Business," *Reason*, October 2005; http://www.reason.com/news/show/32239.htm.

16 Quoted from Genzyme's "Our Commitment," www.genzyme.com/commitment/commitment_home.asp.

17 The business strategist Gary Hamel, with Bill Breen, shows how mission attracts top talent and elicits bigger contributions from people in *The Future of Management* (Boston: Harvard Business School Press, 2007). So too does Bob Willard in his book *The Sustainability Advantage: Seven Business Case Benefits of a Triple Bottom Line* (Gabriola Island, British Columbia, Canada: New Society Publishers, 2002).

18 Howard Schultz and Dori Jones Yang, *Pour Your Heart into It: How Starbucks Built a Company One Cup at a Time* (New York: Hyperion, 1997).

19 Jessica Dicker, "Best Employers, Great Returns," CNNMoney.com, January 18, 2007; http://money.cnn.com/2007/01/17/magazines/fortune/bestcompanies_performance/.

20 Julia Boorstin, "No Preservatives, No Unions, Lots of Dough," *Fortune*, September 15, 2003.

21 Jonah Bloom, "Recession Provides a Chance to Build a Better Capitalism," *Advertising Age*, December 8, 2008.

22 According to the biennial edition, "Report on Socially Responsible Investing Trends in the United States," published by the Social Investment Forum in March 2008.

23 Richard Stengel, with reporting by Jeremy Caplan, "The Responsibility Revolution," *Time*, September 21, 2009.

24 According to the report, "in the 16 of 18 industries examined, companies recognized as sustainably focused outperformed their industry peers over both a three and six-month period, and were well protected from value erosion. Over three months, the performance differential across the 99 companies in this analysis worked out to 10 percent; over six months, the differential was 15 percent."

25 Joe Manget, Catherine Roche, and Felix Münnich, "Capturing the Green Advantage for Consumer Companies," Boston Consulting Group, January 2009.

26 Anthony Ling, Sarah Forrest, Marc Fox, and Stephan Feilhauer, "GS SUSTAIN," Goldman Sachs Global Investment Research, June 2007, p. 5; http://www.unglobalcompact.org/docs/summit2007/gs_esg_embargoed_until030707pdf.pdf.

27 George Pohle and Jeff Hittner, "Attaining Sustainable Growth Through Corporate Responsibility," IBM Institute for Business Value, February 2008.

28 Thomas L. Friedman, "Et Tu, Toyota?" New York Times, October 3, 2007.

29 Felicity Barringer and Andrew Ross Sorkin, "Prominent Green Group to Help Buyout Firm," New York Times, May 1, 2008.

30 "The Seven Sins of Greenwashing: Environmental Claims in Consumer Markets," TerraChoice Environmental Marketing, April 2009.

31 Toby Webb, "Unilever's CEO: Social Innovation and Sustainability the Only Game in Town," Ethical Corporation, May 30, 2007; http://www.ethicalcorporationinstitute.com/.

32 David Roberts, "Energy Efficiency and Sex," Grist, April 29, 2009; http://www.grist.org/article/2009–04–29-energy-efficiency-and-sex.

33 Joseph Pine and James Gilmore, "The End of Corporate Social Responsibility," Harvard Business Publishing, December 26, 2007; http://blogs.harvardbusiness.org/cs/2007/12/the_end_of_corporate_social_re.html.

34 William C. Taylor and Polly LaBarre make a compelling case for "strategy as advocacy" in their book, Mavericks at Work: Why the Most Original Minds in Business Win (New York: William Morrow, 2006).

CHAPTER TWO

1 Portions of this chapter are based on material that first appeared in the following publications: Kermit Pattison, "Wal-Mart Loved Organic Valley's Milk: So Why Cut Off the Flow?" Inc., July 2007; Mike Hughlett, "Volatility in Dairy Business Will Begin to Affect Organic Milk Prices," Chicago Tribune, April 27, 2008; Daniel Franklin, "Just Good Business," The Economist, January 19, 2008; Tricia Holly-Davis, "Can Profits Be Made on Eco Investments?" The Sunday Times (London), April 26, 2009;

Elizabeth Day, "He's the Man Who Gave Marks & Spencer a Life-Saving Makeover," *The Observer* (England), May 31, 2009; Anya Kamenetz, "Ebay's Fair-Trade Marketplace," *Fast Company*, September 17, 2008.

2 Unless otherwise noted, this comment and all others attributed to Organic Valley executives are drawn from interviews conducted by the authors.

3 Quoted from the "Farmers with a Mission" section of Organic Valley's Web site; http://www.organicvalley.coop/our-story/our-cooperative/.

4 Quoted from the "Our Mission" section of Medtronic's Web site; http://www.medtronic.com/about-medtronic/our-mission/.

5 The quote can be found at any number of Ben & Jerry's franchises, including this one in Washington, DC; http://www.dcbenjer.com/.

6 The following articles and books greatly informed our thinking about mission, purpose, and values: former Medtronic CEO Bill George shows how a shared mission and values align people and empower leaders in *True North: Discover Your Authentic Leadership*, written with Peter Sims (San Francisco: Jossey-Bass, 2007); Gary Hamel provides a definitive account of the power of purpose at Whole Foods Market and Google in *The Future of Management*, written with Bill Breen (Boston: Harvard Business School Press, 2007); Rosabeth Moss Kanter demonstrates that mission and values can change even mega-corporations in "Transforming Giants," *Harvard Business Review*, January 1, 2008; http://harvardbusiness.org/product/transforming-giants/an/R0801B-PDF-ENG; in *Mavericks at Work: Why the Most Original Minds in Business Win* (New York: William Morrow, 2006), William C. Taylor and Polly LaBarre put some real brio into the power-of-purpose argument, by showing how it animates outfits like ING Direct USA and the ad agency GSD&M; Mohan Nair convincingly demonstrates that mission yields real motivation in "How Causes Can Animate Companies," *Strategy + Business*, August 28, 2007.

7 Bo Burlingham, "Jim Collins: How to Thrive in 2009," *Inc.*, April 2009; http://www.inc.com/magazine/20090401/in-times-like-these-you-get-a-chance.html.

8 Quoted from the "Sustainability" section of Halliburton's Web site; http://www.halliburton.com/AboutUs/default.aspx?navid=981&pageid=2279.

9 Quoted from the "Environment" section of ExxonMobil's Web site; http://www.exxonmobil.com/corporate/community_environment.aspx.

10 Viktor E. Frankl, *Man's Search for Meaning* (New York: Beacon Press, 1959), p. 122; http://www.webwinds.com/frankl/quotes.htm.

11 James C. Collins and Jerry I. Porras, *Built to Last: Successful Habits of Visionary Companies* (New York: Harper Business, 1994).

12 Kanter's study is expanded in her book *SuperCorp: How Vanguard Companies Create Innovation, Profits, Growth, and Social Good* (New York: Crown Business, 2009).

13 Rosabeth Moss Kanter, "Transforming Giants," *Harvard Business Review*, January 1, 2008; http://harvardbusiness.org/product/transforming-giants/an/R0801B-PDF-ENG.

14 William C. Taylor and Polly LaBarre, *Mavericks at Work: Why the Most Original Minds in Business Win* (New York: William Morrow, 2006).

15 "Organic Valley Culminates 2005 with Launch of 'Generation Organic,'" Organic Valley, December 19, 2005; http://www.organicvalley.coop/newsroom/press-releases/details/article/organic-valley-culminates-2005-with-launch-of-generation-organic.

16 Marjorie Kelly, "Not Just for Profit," *Strategy + Business*, Spring 2009, p. 53.

17 Another data point demonstrating that employee-owned companies deliver outsized performance: in "CoCo Companies: Work, Happiness, and Employee Ownership," a paper published in February 2007 by the UK's Employee Ownership Association, Richard Reeves reports that "The Employees Ownership Index has consistently outperformed [London's] FTSE All-Share. In cash terms, an investment of £100 in the EOI in 1992 would have been worth £349 at the end of June 2003; the same amount invested in the FTSE All-Share would have been worth £161." http://www.employeeownership.co.uk/news%5Cfiles%5C23_1.pdf.

18 Kanter, in "Transforming Giants," presents convincing evidence that even multinational corporations are using values to resolve "long-standing contradictions."

19 Quoted by the journalist and blogger Marc Gunther in his piece, "A Crisis Is a Terrible Thing to Waste," *The Business of Sustainability*; http://www.marcgunther.com/?p=438.

20 Angela Cortez, "Organic Milk Co-ops Respond to Drop in Demand," *Natural Foods Merchandiser*, June 10, 2009; http://naturalfoodsmerchandiser.com/tabId/119/itemId/3894/Organic-milk-coops-respond-to-drop-in-demand.aspx.

21 Unless otherwise noted, this comment and all others attributed to eBay executives are drawn from interviews conducted by the authors.

22 Among Marks and Spencer's many philanthropic efforts: in 2009, employees raised £1.25 million in 125 days for local charities.

23 M&S was one of the pioneers of Business in the Community, a UK-based non-profit that's mobilized more than 850 companies to undertake a sweeping range of worthy initiatives, including closing the gap on gender

pay, disclosing greenhouse-gas emissions, and campaigning for economic renewal in distressed communities; http://www.bitc.org.uk/community/economic_renewal/strategy_and_vision/index.html.

24 The billionaire boss of the British retail company Arcadia Group, Green withdrew his offer after failing to win sufficient backing from shareholders.

25 Unless otherwise noted, this comment and all others attributed to Marks & Spencer executives are drawn from interviews conducted by the authors.

26 As this book went to press, Rose was reportedly planning to step down as chief executive of M&S in July 2010, and stay on as chairman.

27 Sarah Butler, "Shoppers Look Behind the Label to Vote M&S the Greenest," *The (London) Times*, March 28, 2007.

28 "Just Good Business," *The Economist*, January 19, 2008.

29 Joel Makower, "How Bad is Greenwashing, Really?" GreenBiz.com, July 5, 2008; http://www.greenbiz.com/blog/2008/07/06/how-bad-is-greenwashing-really.

30 *Sunday Times*, May 25, 2008.

31 Thomas L. Friedman, *Hot, Flat, and Crowded: Why We Need a Green Revolution—And How It Can Renew America* (New York: Farrar, Straus & Giroux, 2008).

32 According to a report in the *Christian Science Monitor*, roughly 5 to 10 percent of global CO_2 emissions are related to the manufacture and transportation of cement, a major ingredient of concrete. Tony Azios, "Industry Scrambles to Find a 'Greener' Concrete," *Christian Science Monitor*, March 12, 2008; http://www.csmonitor.com/2008/0312/p14s01-stgn.html.

CHAPTER THREE

1 Portions of this chapter are based on material that first appeared in the following publications: Joe Nocera, "The Sinatra of Southwest Feels the Love," *New York Times*, May 24, 2008; Philip Rosedale, as told to Michael Fitzgerald, "How I Did It," *Inc.*, February 2007; Sara Corbett, "Portrait of an Artist as an Avatar," *New York Times*, March 8, 2009; Janet Rae-Dupree, "Even the Giants Can Learn to Think Small," *New York Times*, August 3, 2008; Bill Breen, "The 6 Myths of Creativity," *Fast Company*, December 2004; Jared Sandberg, "A Modern Conundrum: Where Work's Invisible, So Are Its Satisfactions," *Wall Street Journal*, February 19, 2008.

2 On April 16, 2009, Southwest reported a first-quarter loss of $0.03 per share.

3 Katrina Brooker, "The Chairman of the Board Looks Back," *Fortune*, May 28, 2001; http://money.cnn.com/magazines/fortune/fortune_archive/2001/05/28/303852/index.htm.

4 Charles Fishman, "The War for Talent," *Fast Company*, July 1998; http://www.fastcompany.com/magazine/16/mckinsey.html.

5 Articles and books that advanced our thinking about creating a "responsible" workplace: Steffan Stern explores the challenges of "winning the engagement of employees" in "How to Get Staff to Care About Their Work," *Financial Times*, January 31, 2008; Julian Birkinshaw looks at the world through the eyes of "those who are managed"—and it's not a pretty sight—in his article, "What Does It Feel Like to Be Managed?" *Labnotes*, September 2008; Gary Hamel makes a deep, compelling case that companies that are organized around a community model outperform bureaucracies, in *The Future of Management*, written with Bill Breen (Boston: Harvard Business School Press, 2007); the power of the community-based management model is powerfully articulated by Wilbert ("Bill") L. Gore, the founder of W. L. Gore & Associates, in an unpublished paper, "The Lattice Organization—A Philosophy of Enterprise"; we strongly encourage the company to publish Bill Gore's paper.

6 "Closing the Engagement Gap: A Road Map for Driving Superior Business Performance," Towers Perrin Global Workforce Study 2007–2008; http://www.towersperrin.com/tp/getwebcachedoc?webc=HRS/USA/2008/200803/GWS_Global_Report20072008_31208.pdf.

7 "Rethinking Corporate Social Responsibility: A Fleishman-Hillard/National Consumers League Study," May 2007; http://www.csrresults.com/CSR_ExecutiveSummary07.pdf.

8 Gary Hamel with Bill Breen, *The Future of Management* (Boston: Harvard Business School Press, 2007).

9 Julian Birkinshaw, "What Does It Feel Like to Be Managed?" LabNotes, MLab, September, 2008. http://www.managementlab.org/files/LabNotes9.pdf. Birkinshaw is the cofounder, along with Gary Hamel, of MLab (aka the Management Lab), whose mission is to "accelerate the evolution of management."

10 Breen, "The 6 Myths of Creativity"; http://www.fastcompany.com/magazine/89/creativity.html?page=0%2C1.

11 Charles Fishman, "The Anarchist's Cookbook," *Fast Company*, July 2004; http://www.fastcompany.com/magazine/84/wholefoods.html?page=0%2C2.

12 Quoted from "The Company" section of Linden Lab's Web site; http://lindenlab.com/about.

13 Sandberg, "A Modern Conundrum."

14 Unless otherwise noted, this comment and all others attributed to Linden executives are drawn from interviews conducted by the authors.

15 As reported by Corbett, "Portrait of an Artist as an Avatar."

16 Samuel A. Culbert, "Get Rid of the Performance Review!" *Wall Street Journal*, October 20, 2008; http://online.wsj.com/article/SB122426318874844933.html.

17 Rosedale, "How I Did It," *Inc.*, February 2007.

18 Steven Greenhouse, "Working Life (High and Low)," *New York Times*, April 20, 2008.

19 See "About SourceForge.net," http://sourceforge.net/about.

CHAPTER FOUR

1 Among the books and articles that influenced our thinking on transparency, these three stand out: one of the best and most entertaining explorations of transparency's implications for business is Clive Thompson's "The See-Through CEO," *Wired*, March 2007; Don Tapscott and David Ticoll were among the first to spot transparency's ascent in their landmark book, *The Naked Corporation: How the Age of Transparency Will Revolutionize Business* (Free Press, 2003); Shel Holtz and John C. Havens deliver a valuable manual in *Tactical Transparency: How Leaders Can Leverage Social Media to Maximize Value and Build Their Brand* (San Francisco: Jossey-Bass, 2009).

2 Clive Thompson, "The See-Through CEO," *Wired*, March 2007.

3 George Phole and Jeff Hittner, "Attaining Sustainable Growth Through Corporate Social Responsibility," IBM Institute for Business Value, February 2008.

4 Sheila Bonini, Noêmie Brun, and Michelle Rosenthal, "McKinsey Global Survey Results: Valuing Corporate Responsibility," *McKinsey Quarterly*, February 2009; http://www.mckinseyquarterly.com/Valuing_corporate_social_responsibility_McKinsey_Global_Survey_Results_2309.

5 "Edelman Trust Barometer 2009: The Tenth Global Opinion Leaders Survey," Edelman, January 2009.

6 "Edelman Trust Barometer 2009," p. 4.

7 Portions of this chapter are based on material that first appeared in the following publications: Yvon Chouinard, *Let My People Go Surfing: The Education of a Reluctant Businessman* (Penguin Press HC, 2005); *Louder Than Words* (Patagonia, 1999), http://mbianchi.com/docs/louder_than_words.pdf; Lorinda R. Rowledge, Russell S. Barton, and Kevin S. Brady, *Mapping the Journey: Case Studies in Strategy and Action Toward Sustainable Development*, (Greenleaf Publishing, 1999); http://www.greenleaf-publishing.com/content/pdfs/pata.pdf; Alissa Walker, "Measuring Footprints," *Fast Company*, April 2008; http://www.fastcompany.com/magazine/124/measuring-footprints.html; Claudia H. Deutsch, "Seeking a Joint Effort for Greener Athletic Shoes," *New York Times*, September 29,

2007; Heather Green and Kerry Capell, "Carbon Confusion," *BusinessWeek*, March 17, 2008.

8 Susan Casey, "Patagonia: Blueprint for Green Business," *Fortune*, May 29, 2007; http://money.cnn.com/magazines/fortune/fortune_archive/2007/ 04/02/8403423/index.htm.

9 Quoted from "Our Reason for Being" on Patagonia's Web site; http://www.patagonia.com/web/us/patagonia.go?slc=en_US&sct=US& assetid=2047.

10 Unless otherwise noted, this comment and all others attributed to Patagonia executives are drawn from interviews conducted by the authors.

11 Chouinard, *Surfing*, p. 212.

12 Quoted from Lorinda R. Rowledge, Russell S. Barton, and Kevin S. Brady, *Mapping the Journey: Case Studies in Strategy and Action Toward Sustainable Development*, (Greenleaf Publishing, 1999).

13 Chouinard, *Surfing*, p. 205.

14 Jacob Gordon, "The TH Interview: Yvon Chouinard, Founder of Patagonia," *TreeHugger*, February 7, 2008; http://www.treehugger.com/ files/2008/02/the_th_interview_yvon_chouinard.php.

15 Alex Steffen, blogging at WorldChanging, likes Chronicles overall but has a few quibbles; http://www.worldchanging.com/archives//007543.html.

16 Steffen, "The Footprint Chronicles, Grey Matters," WorldChanging, November 8, 2007.

17 "The Timberland Company: 2006 Corporate Social Responsibility Report," Timberland, p. 21; http://www.timberland.com/include/csr_ reports/2006_TBL_CSR_Report_Full.pd.

18 Quoted from a presentation that Rick Ridgeway gave on November 17, 2008 at the "Opportunity Green: 2008" conference held at UCLA. Video of Ridgeway's talk is posted on "Melodies in Marketing," http://www.melodiesinmarketing.com/2008/11/17/the-patagonia-story-rick-ridgeway/.

19 See the "Transparency & Accountability" section of Timberland's Web site, http://www.timberland.com/corp/index.jsp?page=../include/ csr_reports.

20 Unless otherwise noted, this comment and all others attributed to Timberland and Novo Nordisk executives are drawn from interviews conducted by the authors.

21 Thomas L. Friedman, "9/11 and 4/11," *New York Times*, July 20, 2008; http://www.nytimes.com/2008/07/20/opinion/20friedman.html.

22 Simon Zadek, "The Path to Corporate Responsibility," *Harvard Business Review*, December 1, 2004.

23 "European Convention for the Protection of Vertebrate Animals Used for Experimental and Other Scientific Purposes," Council of Europe, December 2, 2005.
24 Quoted from Miguel Bustillo, "Wal-Mart to Assign New 'Green' Ratings," *Wall Street Journal*, July 16, 2009.

CHAPTER FIVE
1 Portions of this chapter are based on material that first appeared in the following publications: Nicholas Ind, "Patagonia: The World's Most Authentic Brand?" Glasshouse Partnership; http://www.glasshousepartnership .com/downloads/nicholas-ind-on-patagonia-and-brand-authenticity.pdf; Lorinda R. Rowledge, Russell S. Barton, and Kevin S. Brady, *Mapping the Journey: Case Studies in Strategy and Action Toward Sustainable Development* (Greenleaf Publishing, 1999); Yvon Chouinard, *Let My People Go Surfing: The Education of a Reluctant Businessman* (New York: Penguin Press, 2005); Eugenia Levenson, "Citizen Nike," *Fortune*, November 17, 2008; Thomas W. Malone, Wanda J. Orlikowski, and Peter M. Senge, "In Praise of the Incomplete Leader," *Harvard Business Review*, February 2007; Simon Zadek, "The Path to Corporate Responsibility," *Harvard Business Review*, December 2004; Bill Breen, "Who Do You Love?" *Fast Company*, May 2007; "A Stitch in Time," *The Economist*, January 19, 2008; Richard Locke, Fei Qin, and Alberto Brause, "Does Monitoring Improve Labor Standards? Lessons from Nike," MIT Sloan Working Paper No. 4612–06, MIT Sloan School of Management, July 2006; Reena Jana, "Quality Over Green," *BusinessWeek*, January 28, 2008.
2 Thomas Friedman, "Et Tu, Toyota?" *New York Times*, October 3, 2007.
3 John Grant, *The New Marketing Manifesto: The 12 Rules for Building Successful Brands in the 21st Century* (Texere Publishing, 2000).
4 Among the recent spate of books on authenticity that contributed to our understanding, these three stand out: David Boyle does a masterful job of exploring the line between fake and real in *Authenticity: Brands, Fakes, Spin, and the Lust for Real Life* (Harper Perennial, 2003); James H. Gilmore and B. Joseph Pine II limn the "appeal of real" for consumers—and what that means for companies—in *Authenticity: What Consumers Really Want* (Harvard Business School Press, 2007); and Richard Florida, in his landmark book *The Rise of the Creative Class: And How It's Transforming Work, Leisure, Community, and Everyday Life* (Basic Books, 2002), shows how the search for the authentic influences where cultural creatives live and work, and what they buy.
5 David Boyle, *Authenticity*.
6 Gilmore and Pine, *Authenticity: What Consumers Really Want*.

7 "The Six Sins of Greenwashing: A Study of Environmental Claims in North American Consumer Markets," TerraChoice Environmental Marketing, November 2007; http://www.terrachoice.com/files/6_sins.pdf.

8 Joseph Romm, "BP Joins 'Biggest Global Warming Crime Ever Seen,'" Grist, December 19, 2007; http://www.grist.org/article/proof-that-beyond-petroleum-was-greenwashing.

9 Brian Stelter, "When Chevron Hires Ex-Reporter to Investigate Pollution, Chevron Looks Good," New York Times, May 11, 2009.

10 John J. Fialka, "As It Polishes Green Image, GE Fights EPA," Wall Street Journal, February 13, 2007.

11 Ben Elgin, "Green—Up to a Point," BusinessWeek, March 3, 2008.

12 Vesela Veleva, "Time to Get Real: Closing the Gap Between Rhetoric and Reality," Boston College Center for Corporate Citizenship, December 2007; http://www.bcccc.net/index.cfm?fuseaction=document.showDocumentByID&DocumentID=1172.

13 Michael E. Porter and Mark R. Kramer, "Strategy and Society: The Link Between Competitive Advantage and Corporate Social Responsibility," Harvard Business Review, December 1, 2006; http://harvardbusiness.org/product/strategy-and-society-the-link-between-competitive-/an/R0612D-PDF-ENG.

14 Nicholas Ind, "Patagonia: The World's Most Authentic Brand?"

15 For example, see Lorinda R. Rowledge, Russell S. Barton, and Kevin S. Brady, Mapping the Journey: Case Studies in Strategy and Action Toward Sustainable Development.

16 Chouinard, Surfing.

17 Nicholas Ind, "Inside Out," Propeller, 2002; http://www.nicholasind.com/articles/articles_insideout.html.

18 Chouinard, Surfing.

19 Unless noted otherwise, this comment and all others attributed to Patagonia executives are drawn from interviews conducted by the authors.

20 To learn more about impact investing, see Jessica Freireich and Katherine Fulton, "Investing for Social & Environmental Impact: A Design for Catalyzing an Emerging Industry," Monitor Institute, January 2009; http://www.monitorinstitute.com/impactinvesting/documents/InvestingforSocialandEnvImpact_FullReport_004.pdf. The report tracks how "profit-seeking investment to generate social and environmental good is moving from a periphery of activist investors to the core of mainstream financial institutions."

21 Unless noted otherwise, this comment and all others attributed to Nike executives are drawn from interviews conducted by the authors.

22 Zadek, "Path to Corporate Responsibility."

23 Richard M. Locke, "The Promise and Perils of Globalization: The Case of Nike," teaching case for the Sloan School of Management.

24 Kim Mackrael, "A Natural Step Case Study: Nike," *The Natural Step*, January 2009; http://www.thenaturalstep.org/sites/all/files/Nike%20Case%20Study_Jan2009.pdf.

CHAPTER SIX

1 Portions of this chapter are based on material that first appeared in the following publications: Josh Bernoff and Charlene Li, "Harnessing the Power of the Oh-So-Social Web," *MIT Sloan Management Review*, April 1, 2008; Max Chafkin, "The Customer Is the Company," *Inc.*, June 2008; Clive Thompson, "The Revolution in Micromanufacturing," *Wired*, February 2009; Rob Walker, "Handmade 2.0," *New York Times Magazine*, December 16, 2007; Linda Tischler, "The Fast 50: Etsy," *Fast Company*, February 2009; Pan Kwan Yuk, "A Business Crafted for Artisans," *The Financial Times*, February 26, 2008; Jessi Hempel, "Big Blue Brainstorm," *BusinessWeek*, August 7, 2006; Steve Hamm, "Thinking the Future," *BusinessWeek*, March 9, 2006; Ian Williams, "IBM Makes a Splash in Water Technology," BusinessGreen.com, March 16, 2009.

2 Mary Pilon, "Credit Cards Get the Ax—and Blender," *Wall Street Journal*, June 18, 2009.

3 The term "plastectomy" was reportedly coined by Dave Ramsey, a radio talk show host with Fox Business News.

4 Bernoff and Li, "Harnessing the Power of the Oh-So-Social Web."

5 These and other examples of customers leveraging the Web to fight back are chronicled in Charlene Li and Josh Bernoff's *Groundswell: Winning in a World Transformed by Social Technologies* (Boston: Harvard Business School Press, 2008).

6 Shoshana Zuboff and James Maxmin, *The Support Economy: Why Corporations are Failing Individuals and the Next Episode of Capitalism* (New York: Penguin Books, 2002).

7 Over the past decade, few business concepts have had as much appeal as co-creation and open innovation. Some of the most insightful explorations of democratic idea generation and production: James Surowiecki convincingly shows how groups are sometimes smarter than the smartest person in them in his classic book *The Wisdom of Crowds* (New York: Random House, 2004); Don Tapscott and Anthony D. Williams were also among the first to spot the rise of collective knowledge as a force for egalitarian creation in their groundbreaking book *Wikinomics: How Mass Collaboration Changes Everything* (New York: Portfolio, 2006); two more recent books powerfully demonstrate the implications of mass collaboration and social

media for business: Jeff Howe, *Crowdsourcing: Why the Power of the Crowd Is Driving the Future of Business* (New York: Crown Business, 2008), and the aforementioned Li and Bernoff's *Groundswell.*

8 Working Assets' cell-phone company is marketed under the CREDO Mobile brand.

9 Over the years, Working Assets' customers have supported the ACLU, Greenpeace, Doctors Without Borders, and the Organic Consumers Association, among many other groups.

10 Max Chafkin, "The Customer Is the Company," *Inc.*, June 2008.

11 Michael Tomasello, "How Are Humans Unique?" *New York Times Magazine*, May 25, 2008, p. 15.

12 This point, as well as a deeper exploration of the origins of "Etsy," can be found at "Et si," The Name Inspector, http://www.thenameinspector .com/etsy/.

13 Unless otherwise noted, this comment and all others attributed to Etsy executives come from interviews with the authors.

14 As this book was going to press, Etsy moved into new offices and, according to CEO Thomas, had "developed a comprehensive office ecology plan to establish Etsy as a strong advocate for green principles."

15 Quoted from Slow Food's "Our Philosophy," http://www.slowfood.com/ about_us/eng/philosophy.lasso.

16 Rob Walker, "Handmade 2.0," *New York Times Magazine*, December 16, 2007.

17 Clive Thompson, "The Revolution in Micromanufacturing," *Wired*, March 2009.

18 Clive Thompson makes this point in "The Revolution in Micromanufacturing."

19 Jessica Bruder, "The Etsy Wars," *Fortune Small Business*, July 15, 2009.

20 Quoted from the video clip "GreenXchange," http://sciencecommons .org/projects/greenxchange/.

21 Agnes Mazur, "GreenXchange: Creating a Meta-Map of Sustainability," NaturalPath, May 5, 2009; http://www.naturalpath.com/sustainability/ green-xchange-creating-meta-map-sustainability.

22 "Deep Dive Briefing Material: Water and the Oceans," IBM Global Innovation Outlook, Atlanta, September 23, 2008.

23 Ariel Schwartz, "Big Blue Sees Green, Plunges into Water Management," *Fast Company*, March 13, 2009; http://www.fastcompany.com/blog/ariel- schwartz/sustainability/ibm-plunges-water-management.

24 "Global Innovation Outlook 2.0," IBM Global Innovation Outlook, March 2006; http://www.ibm.com/ibm/gio/media/pdf/GIO_06_Book_ SnglPgs_zz.pdf.

25 Richard R. Ellsworth, *Leading with Purpose: The New Corporate Realities* (Palo Alto: Stanford Business Books, 2002), p. 115.

26 Ellsworth, *Leading with Purpose*.

27 Unless otherwise noted, this comment and all others attributed to IBM executives come from interviews with the authors.

CHAPTER SEVEN

1 Reich makes a powerful, though ultimately unpersuasive, case for this view in his provocative book *Supercapitalism: The Transformation of Business, Democracy, and Everyday Life* (New York: Knopf, 2007).

2 Quoted from Elspeth Cisneros, "Robert Reich, Supercapitalism," *Prosper*, December 2007; http://www.prospermag.com/article/283–160.

3 A point that's made in Wikipedia's definition of "corporation"; http://en.wikipedia.org/wiki/Corporation.

4 Marjorie Kelly, *The Divine Right of Capital: Dethroning the Corporate Aristocracy* (San Francisco: Berrett-Koehler, 2001); http://p2pfoundation.net/Divine_Right_of_Capital.

5 Much of this discussion is drawn from Seventh Generation's work with Carol Sanford and our interviews with her. Connect with Carol at http://carolsanford.com/index.htm.

6 We highly recommend Peter M. Senge, C. Otto Scharmer, Joseph Jaworski, and Betty Sue Flowers, *Presence: An Exploration of Profound Change in People, Organizations, and Society* (New York: Doubleday Publishing/Society for Organizational Learning, 2005).

7 From Carol Sanford's Web site, http://carolsanford.com/about.htm.

8 David Brooks, "The Power of Posterity," *New York Times*, July 28, 2009.

9 Jeff Bezos, Julia Kirby, and Thomas A. Stewart, "The Institutional Yes: An Interview with Jeff Bezos," *Harvard Business Review*, October 1, 2007.

10 For a vivid description of how completely Sam Walton's "presence" continues to permeate Wal-Mart, see Charles Fishman's excellent book *The Wal-Mart Effect: How the World's Most Powerful Company Really Works—and How It's Transforming the American Economy* (New York: Penguin, 2006).

11 In 2004, Seventh Generation won the Small Business Corporate Stewardship Award, which is given to the nation's best example of corporate citizenship among small enterprises. That same year, *Fast Company* magazine picked Seventh Generation as one of its "Fast 50: The World's Most Innovative Companies;" a coalition of New England's transportation and environmental organizations selected Seventh Generation as one of New England's "best workplaces for commuters"; and the Minnesota-based Alliance for Sustainability honored Seventh Generation for "great accomplishment" across a wide range of sustainability endeavors. Also

that year, Vermont Business for Social Responsibility awarded Jeffrey Hollender its Terry Ehrich Award "for having created a business model that encompasses a healthy and productive workplace, welcomes and promotes flexibility for employees, and has a key focus on the importance of life-friendly policies."

12 In 1966, Charles Krone developed the Task Cycle for Procter & Gamble's Lima, Ohio, manufacturing business. In the early 1970s, Krone and Carol Sanford used the Task Cycle with DuPont, as well as many other companies in the following decades. Sanford, with permission, developed an augmented version of the Cycle for Seventh Generation.

13 Seventh Generation's mission is "to inspire a more conscious and sustainable world by being an authentic force for positive change."

14 Seventh Generation's Revised Global Imperatives (June 2009):

provide regenerative & effective product solutions
we develop household and personal care products that delight and systemically regenerate the health and wellbeing of our consumers and our environment.

restore our environment
we ensure that natural resources are used at a rate that is always below their rate of depletion. We will actively contribute to repairing the damage and ensure the raw materials we use are regenerative of the world's natural systems.

build coalitions that create new possibilities
no one can solve the challenges we face alone; we must set aside what divides us and come together around our common responsibility to future generations to generate systemic solutions and brighter possibilities.

create a just and equitable world
we believe happy, healthy people make the world a better place; we will create a just and equitable world through the marketplace. We will proudly "give back" by volunteering our time, our knowledge and by donating 10% of our profits to support organizations working for positive change.

inspire conscious consumption
holding the past, the present, and the future in the same mind, we will create a world rich in values as contrasted to a world rich in artifacts. We're dedicated to being "provisioners" of greater consumer consciousness and personal development through dialogue and education that encourages people to understand how their decisions today impact the next seven generations.

15 According to the Environmental Working Group.

16 According to the Roundtable on Sustainable Palm Oil, http://www
    .rspo.org/resource_centre/RSPO_Presentation_Basic.ppt. An article in
    the *New York Times* reports that 40% of the products on Australian
    supermarket shelves contain palm oil; http://www.nytimes.com/2009/
    09/10/business/energy-environment/10palm.html?pagewanted=2.

17 Greenpeace reports that Indonesia's place as one of the planet's top three
    greenhouse gas emitters is driven largely by deforestation; http://www
    .greenpeace.org.uk/forests/palm-oil.

ACKNOWLEDGMENTS

This book builds on a foundation of innovation from both thought leaders and practitioners, as well as organizations that have supported the evolution of this new way of doing business, and the customers and consumers who made it all possible. Whatever the book's shortcomings, they belong to us. Whatever its merit, the credit goes to the following:

We have attempted to show how a new breed of responsible companies is leveraging some of the best thinking on management, strategy, leadership, and innovation. Much of that best thinking—and best storytelling—comes from Gary Hamel, Peter Senge, Rosabeth Moss Kanter, Teresa Amabile, Simon Zadek, Don Tapscott, Charlene Li and Josh Bernoff, Shoshana Zuboff and James Maxmin, and Carol Sanford. We are grateful to each of these individuals for casting a light into the future and showing us the way.

The Responsibility Revolution has emerged, and is now converging into a global community. Without the willingness of innovators and leaders at companies in the U.S. and Europe to open their doors to us and share their stories, we could never have written this book. We are grateful for their generosity toward us, but more importantly, their desire to reinvent what it means for a corporation to truly be "responsible."

We therefore wish to acknowledge the following companies and individuals: at Triodos Bank: Peter Blom, Hans Schut, and Marilou van Golstein Brouwers; at Organic Valley Family of Farms: George Siemon, Theresa Marquez, and Jim Wedeberg; at eBay: John Donahoe and Robert Chatwani; at World of Good: Pryia Haji; at Marks & Spencer: Mike Barry and Richard Gillies; at Linden Lab: Philip Rosedale, Adreanne Radonich, Chris Collins, and Mark Kingdon; and at Seventh Generation: Susan Johnson, Garry Embleton, John LeBourveau, Reed Doyle, Dave Rapaport, Ashley Orgain, and Tim Fowler; at Patagonia: Yvon Chouinard, Rick Ridgeway, Casey Sheahan, and Jill Dumain; at Novo Nordisk: Lise Holst; at Working Assets: Laura Scher; at Timberland: Jeffrey Swartz, Beth Holzman, Betsy Blaidsell, and Colleen Von Haden; at B Corp: Jay Coen Gilbert and Andrew Kassoy; at Nike: Mark Parker, Hannah Jones, Lorrie Vogel, and Sarah Severn; at Etsy.com: Maria Thomas, Mary Andrews, and Matthew Stinchcomb; at IBM: David Yaun, Ed Bevan, Mark Harris, and Kris Lichter; at Cisco: Marthin De Beer; at St. Luke's advertising agency: Neil Henderson; and at Gap Inc.: Dan Henkle and Kindley Walsh-Lawlor.

Then there is the team that made this book. Our literary agent, Christy Fletcher, is a true woman-warrior who found a home for the book just days before giving birth to her daughter. And we thank Peter M. Senge for graciously agreeing to write a foreword for this work.

We are indebted to Jossey-Bass for giving us the chance to partner with its incredible staff. In the book, we argue that energy sparks innovation; Jossey-Bass has one of the most caffeinated crews in publishing. Karen Murphy, our editor, gave us the freedom to create and the guidance to find true north. Her enthusiasm was always welcome; her suggestions were invariably on target. The energy that came from Erin Moy and her marketing colleagues—Cynthia Shannon, Nick Snider, and Bernadette Blanco—was a huge boon to our efforts. We are grateful to the design/production team—Mark Karmendy and Adrian

Morgan—for turning our words into this book. And we are very appreciative of Kristi Hein's deft copy editing.

Finally, we'd like to make a few personal acknowledgments.

From Jeffrey: My thinking was shaped by some of my earliest teachers, including Wilson Alling, David Sundaram, David Levine, Marc Vahanian, Gregor Barnum, Peter Graham, the late Anita Roddick, Ben Cohen, Peter Barnes, Michael Kieschnick, Lisa Scher, Marshall McLuhan, R. D. Lang, Ivan Illich, and my original partner in Seventh Generation, Alan Newman.

Without the lessons, learning, and total support of the entire Seventh Generation community, none of my work would be possible. Special thanks goes to Lee Pelletier, who takes special care of me every day.

While many organizations have supported the responsible business community, none have played a more central role than the leaders of the Social Venture Network (SVN): Josh Mailman, Richard Perl, Wayne Silby, Joel Solomon, and Joe Sibilia. SVN was the incubator out of which so many leading responsible businesses evolved.

I also owe a huge debt of gratitude to Peter Victor, Allen White, Gar Alperovitz , Jonathan Porritt, Muhammad Yunus, Peter M. Senge, C. Otto Scharmer, Joseph Jaworski, Betty S. Flowers, Riane Eisler, Janine Benyus, Paul Hawken, Amory Lovins and L. Hunter Lovins, John Elkington, Simon Zadek, Herman E. Daly, Lynn Sharp Paine, Gus Speth, Joel Makower, Bill McKibben, Ray Anderson, Gary Erickson, Tom Newmark, Deb Nelson, Pamela Chaloult, Aaron Kramer, Mindy Lubber and Robert Massey, Liz Maw, John Passacantando, Steven Viederman, and Frances Moore-Lappé.

From Bill: Thanks to my colleagues at Seventh Generation for welcoming me into their fold and giving me an inside look at how purpose shapes strategy. I also want to thank the cofounders of *Fast Company*, Alan Webber and Bill Taylor, for creating such an inspiring and fulfilling place to work. That adventure is over, but the thrill will always remain. I am indebted to my longtime *Fast Company* colleague, Charles Fishman, for his generosity and infectious curiosity.

As for Lise, your first-draft edits set me straight and your unvarnished feedback kept me going. You were a true and most-valuable partner through every moment of writing this book.

Jeffrey Hollender and Bill Breen
February 2010

ABOUT THE
AUTHORS

Jeffrey Hollender is the cofounder, executive chairman, and chief inspired protagonist of Seventh Generation, the nation's leading brand of natural household and personal-care products. He is a director of Greenpeace USA, Vermont Businesses for Social Responsibility, and Alloy Media & Marketing, and a member and former director of the Social Venture Network. He is the cofounder of Community Capital Bank, a New York financial institution that invests in affordable housing and community development.

Hollender frequently addresses social and environmental responsibility issues at regional, national, and international venues, including the World Economic Forum, the Harvard Environmental Forum, the National Press Club, the Green Festival, the World Resources Institute, Nike Apparel Group, the Environmental Protection Agency, the United Nations Summit on Sustainable Growth, and the Businesses for Social Responsibility national conference. He is the author of two best-selling books, *How to Make the World a Better Place: A Guide for Doing Good* (WW Norton) and *What Matters Most: How a Small Group of Pioneers Is Teaching Social Responsibility to Big Business, and Why Big Business Is Listening* (Basic Books), as well as *Naturally Clean: The Seventh Generation*

Guide to Safe & Healthy, Non-Toxic Cleaning (New Society Publishers), and *In Our Every Deliberation; Seventh Generation: The Journey Toward Corporate Consciousness* (BookSurge Publishing). You can find Jeffrey through his blog, www.inspiredprotagonist.com.

———————

Bill Breen is the editorial director of Seventh Generation, where he leads writing and editing initiatives for the company's publishing activities. He is the coauthor, with the business strategist Gary Hamel, of *The Future of Management* (Harvard Business School Press), which Amazon.com selected as the best business book of 2007. As senior editor, Breen was a member of the founding team that launched *Fast Company*, which gained an avid following among innovators and business leaders and won numerous awards, including the National Magazine Award for General Excellence. During his twelve-year tenure at *Fast Company*, he edited the magazine's sections on personal success as well as special issues on design and leadership, and wrote many articles on strategy, innovation, and competition.

Breen speaks to business audiences throughout the country on leadership, innovation, and connecting strategy with sustainability; he has appeared on CNN, Fox, CBS, National Public Radio, and other media outlets. He lives with his wife, daughter, and son in Gloucester, Massachusetts; connect with Bill at bbreen@billbreen.net.

INDEX

207